Basic English for Architecture
—Listening & Speaking—

建築を学ぶ人のための総合英語
—リスニング&スピーキング—

Emiko Hirose Horton
Masa Horikawa Tsuneyasu
Cecilia Smith Fujishima
Hanako Kamiya

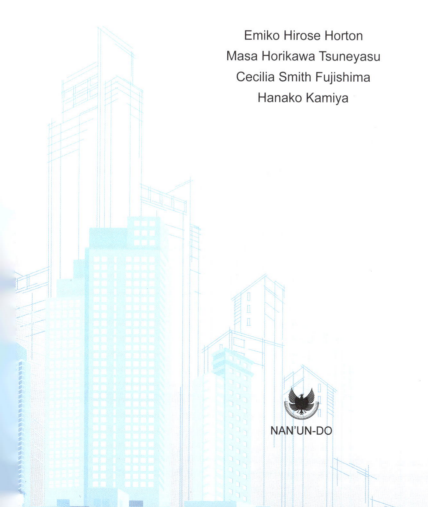

NAN'UN-DO

Basic English for Architecture
—Listening & Speaking—

Copyright© 2019

by
Emiko Hirose Horton
Masa Horikawa Tsuneyasu
Cecilia Smith Fujishima
Hanako Kamiya

All Rights Reserved
No part of this book may be reproduced in any form without written permission from the authors and Nan'un-do Co., Ltd.

はしがき

　本書は建築系を学ぶ、あるいは建築系の仕事に携わり始めた学習者のための語学（英語）学習テキストです。建築系の学修／実務で必要な語彙の習得と表現を中心とした 12 ユニットで構成されています。全ユニットを通して、ひとつのプロジェクトチームとクライアントが建築・建築工学・都市計画・環境などに関連する会話をしていく設定で組まれています。

　グローバル化が進む中、それぞれの分野においての英語運用能力が求められており、ESP (English for Specific Purposes) の重要性と必要性が認められています。しかし、実際に専門分野に関連した語彙や表現、そして想定されるセッティングにおける会話練習を提供する授業教材としての英語テキストは多くはありません。EGP (English for General Purposes)・EAP (English for Academic Purposes) として作成されたテキストは、その目的から非常に広い範囲のトピックを含んでいます。しかし、限られた学習時間の中で建築関連場面での「使える英語」の力を付けるためには、その分野に特化した語彙を強化し、コミュニケーション力をつけるための学習が必要となります。また、建築関連企業でも新入社員の英語力は課題の一つとなっているという声も聞こえてきます。本書は、建築系の大学生および企業における語学研修で使える入門レベルの建築系英語テキストを目指しました。学習者のターゲットとしてはTOEIC400 点～ 500 点レベルを設定していますが、スクリプトの使用や授業内アクティビティを取り入れることで、設定レベルよりも低いあるいは高いレベルのクラスでの使用も可能です。

各ユニットは、以下のように構成されています。

Vocabulary: 　ユニットの会話や Grammar point で出てくる語彙を学習します。また、関連する語彙をさらに More vocabulary で学ぶことが出来ます。

Pronunciation: 　特に日本人の英語学習者にとって弱点ともいえる音などをピックアップしました。発音の練習をすることはリスニング力をアップするにも効果的です。

Grammar Point: 　細かい文法説明ではなく、どのような時に使うのかといった機能的側面から文法を復習します。

Conversation: 　Conversation 1 は会話練習用です。Vocabulary ／ More Vocabulary で学んだ語彙が含まれた会話の練習をします。Conversation 2 では聞き取り練習をします。会話は少し長いですが、Comprehension Questions を見ながら繰り返し聞くことで耳を鳴らしていきます。

　各ユニットの最後には GOOD TO KNOW という短い読み物を入れました。コミュニケーション関連のことあるいは建築関連の「豆知識」的なものとなっています。

　Teacher's manual では、アクティブな授業とするための授業内活動のアイディアも紹介しています。より楽しく、将来の建築系の学習や仕事に役立つ授業となるような英語教材を目指しました。多くの人がより専門的な学習に進んでいく準備の一助になれば幸いです。

　なお、本書の執筆にあたり、芝浦工業大学建築学部の伊藤洋子教授、隈澤文俊教授には、構成や内容等で大変貴重なアドバイスや確認をいただきました。感謝申し上げます。

CONTENTS

Unit 1
INTRODUCTION: Introducing the project team   07

Unit 2
PLANNING : Talking about the project site   13

Unit 3
FLOOR PLAN: Talking about the rooms   19

Unit 4
BUILDING STRUCTURE: 25
Talking about building structure and materials

Unit 5
KITCHEN: Talking about kitchen design and appliances   31

Unit 6
DINING & LIVING ROOM: Talking about furniture   37

Unit 7
    DESIGN & STYLE: Talking about windows and lighting   43

Unit 8
    SCALE & DIMENSION: 49
    Talking about sizes and shapes of furniture

Unit 9
    COLORS & MATERIALS: 55
    Talking about preferences in colors and materials

Unit 10
    SUSTAINABLE DESIGN: 61
    Talking about environmentally friendly designs

Unit 11
    NATURAL HAZARDS: 67
    Talking about protecting buildings from natural hazards

Unit 12
    URBAN DESIGN: 73
    Talking about infrastructure planning

Unit 1
INTRODUCTION: Introducing the project team

OBJECTIVES

Vocabulary: To learn the names of different professions in architecture
Pronunciation: To learn the importance of word stress
Grammar: To explain things using relative pronouns
Conversation: To introduce the project members

Vocabulary

1 Match the words and the meanings.

1. owner/client [ ]
2. architect [ ]
3. contractor [ ]
4. civil engineer [ ]
5. landscape architect [ ]
6. structural engineer [ ]
7. plumbing engineer [ ]
8. electrical engineer [ ]
9. Interior designer [ ]
10. allow [ ]
11. outlet [ ]
12. column [ ]

a. ランドスケープデザイナー　b. 〜を可能にする　c. 土木技術者　d. インテリアデザイナー
e. 建築主；施主　f. 構造設計者　g. 電気設備設計者　h. 給排水設備設計者
i. コンセント　j. 契約者；請負業者　k. 柱　l. 建築設計者

2 Which engineer is talking? Match the talk 1~6 and the words a~f below.

1. ( ) "This method allows the floor to have fewer pillars."
2. ( ) "I will make sure that all the sections of the construction come together smoothly."
3. ( ) "I don't think three outlets are enough for the bedroom."
4. ( ) "This system allows the easy adjustment of water temperature."
5. ( ) "The outside areas should have easy access for the residents."
6. ( ) "We are building a new bridge for the town."

a. plumbing engineer
b. architect
c. structural engineer
d. electrical engineer
e. landscape engineer
f. civil engineer

【More Words】

mechanical engineer 設備技術者, kitchen designer キッチン・デザイナー, lighting designer 照明デザイナー, land surveyor 土地の測量士・測量業者, environmental consultant 環境コンサルタント, manufacturer 製造業者、メーカー, plumber 配管工・業者, electrical 電気の, landscape 景観、ランドスケープ, temperature 温度, construction 工事, method 方法・技法, resident 住人, residential 住宅の, surveyor 調査員, abbreviation 省略形、略語, scale 規模, briefly 簡単に, firm 会社, reinforced concrete 鉄筋コンクリート, pillar 柱

Some Abbreviations:
OAC: (Owner, Architect, and Contractor) They have a weekly OAC meeting.
MEP: (Mechanical, Electrical, and Plumbing engineer)
PLUMB: Plumbing　　　MTL: Metal　　　INT: Interior　　　FLR: Floor

PRONUNCIATION

1 Pay attention to the vowel with primary stress indicated in bold. Practice the pronunciation of the words using the CD.

1. **o**wner
2. cl**i**ent
3. **a**rchitect
4. c**i**vil
5. pl**u**mbing
6. el**e**ctrical
7. c**o**ntractor
8. engin**ee**r
9. int**e**rior
10. l**a**ndscape
11. prot**e**ction
12. des**i**gner

2 Listen to the CD and put a stress-mark (′) above the vowel with the strongest stressed vowel in each word below.

1. allow
2. temperature
3. construction
4. outlets
5. bedroom
6. method
7. project
8. access
9. residents
10. surveyor
11. consultant
12. elevator
13. manufacturer
14. security
15. abbreviation

GRAMMAR POINT

Relative Pronouns

物や人について説明・描写してみよう：Explaining/describing things/people using *relative pronouns*（関係代名詞）

関係詞（who, whose, whom, which, that）は2つの文を1つにつなげる働きをします。ここでは主に主格の役割を復習しましょう。主格の関係代名詞は、それが何なのか／その人はどのような人なのか等について、関係代名詞で繋げた文が後ろから先行詞を修飾する働きをします。who は人の場合、which は人以外、そして that は人と人以外のどちらの場合でも用いることができます。先行詞が only, very や最上級の形容詞によって修飾されている場合や先行詞が nothing, all などの場合、関係代名詞は that が好まれることが多いです。

先行詞・格	主格	所有格	目的格
人	who	whose	whom/who
動物・事物	which	whose/of which	which
人・動物・事物	that	—	that

基本的な手順は (1) 2つの文で同じ人、動物、事物を見つける、(2) 片方の名詞を関係代名詞に置き換える、(3) 先行詞後に関係代名詞が来るように残りの文を置く。

Unit 1

例 1

(1) I have a friend. He is an electrical engineer.

(2) a friend と He が同一人物です。who を使用します。

(3) I have a friend **who** is an electrical engineer.

例 2

(1) John is working at a big interior design firm. It is a five-minute walk from the station.

(2) a big interior design firm と It が同一物です。which/that を使用します。

(3) John is working at a big interior design firm **which/that** is a five-minute walk from the station.

1 Complete the sentences using the words in parentheses.

1. その家をデザインした建築家は日本語を話せます。

   The architect (the, can, designed, house, Japanese, who, speak).

   _____.

2. スタンは小・中規模の住宅プロジェクトに取組む方が好きです。

   Stan prefers to work on residential projects (medium, which, small, are, scale, or).

   _____.

3. 私の姉はニューヨークで働く電気設備設計士です。

   My sister is an electrical engineer (works, N.Y., who, in).

   _____.

4. 彼は今日の午後1時に請負業者と会う約束があります。

   He has an appointment with the contractor (project, who, working, is, on, the) at 1 p.m. today.

   _____.

5. あの教授は自然の光が入ってくる教室をいつも好んで使用します。

   That professor usually uses classrooms (light, that, get, natural).

   _____.

Conversation 1

1 Practice the conversation in pairs or groups.

Mika (Architect): Thank you for coming, Tom.

Tom (Client): Hi, Mika. I'm excited that your team is working on my new project.

Mika: Thanks. Me too. Let me introduce the members.
This is Brian, the structural engineer; Sherry, the interior designer; Ed, the plumbing engineer; Cindy, the landscape designer, and Stan, the kitchen designer. Everybody, this is Mr. Tom Rogers, our client and the owner of the property.

Tom: Thank you for making time for me today. Could you briefly tell me about yourselves, starting from Brian?

Brian (Structural engineer): Of course. I've been working as a structural engineer for the past 18 years. Five years ago I started my own company. Mika and I have worked together on projects for many years.

2 **Pair Work:** Using the information below, practice introducing yourself as one of the team members.

Sherry: has been working as an interior designer for 10 years. She owns an interior designing office and has designed many houses and shops. Last year, she won an Excellent Interior Award.

Ed: has been working as a plumbing engineer for 25 years. He specializes in residential plumbing systems. His shop has a 24-hour emergency line, and he has many customers in this town.

Cindy: has been working as a landscape designer for 12 years. She designs small gardens to large parks. She just finished designing the garden of the building next door.

Stan: has been working as a kitchen designer for 8 years. One of his projects was introduced in the magazine *Best Kitchen*. His own kitchen is a country-style kitchen.

Example conversation:

Student A: Hello. I'm _____, _____. Nice to meet you.

Student B: Hi, I'm Tom. Glad to meet you. How long have been a/an _____?

Student A: I've been working as a/an _____ for _____ years.

Student B: Mika told me that you _____.

Student A: Yes, that's right.

Student B: That's great. I'm very happy to have you on the project team.

Conversation 2

Listen to the rest of the conversation. Write all the words you can hear. Compare and discuss with your partner. 06

Memo

1 Listen to the conversation again and write T if the statement is true or F if false.
1. Brian is the president of Mika's company. (   )
2. Sherry, who is doing the interiors, has worked with the client before. (   )
3. Sherry is currently working with Mika. (   )
4. Ed only works on apartments. (   )
5. Stan likes working with Mika. (   )

2 Listen to the conversation again and fill in the blanks below.
1. Brian is an expert in wood, metal, and _____ construction.
2. Sherry is now working on a _____ housing project.
3. Ed has been working as a plumbing engineer for _____ years.
4. Stan is planning to make the kitchen a _____ of the project.

11

GOOD TO KNOW

Introducing People

In a business setting, it is important to pay attention to how you introduce people. At the first meeting between your project team and the client, start by giving the names of your team members first, then give the client's name after that. Look at the examples below.

"Mr. /Ms. Client, this is Ed, the plumbing engineer of our team. Ed, this is Mr. /Ms. Client"
OR
"Mr. /Ms. Client, this is Ed. Ed, this is Mr. Cient."

Unit 2
PLANNING : Talking about the project site

OBJECTIVES

Vocabulary: To learn words related to a local area
Pronunciation: To practice linked sounds
Grammar: To describe locations using prepositions
Conversation: To talk about an area and a project site

Vocabulary

1 Match the words and the meanings.

1. site [　]
2. laundromat [　]
3. public facility [　]
4. block [　]
5. familiar with [　]
6. next to [　]
7. parking lot [　]
8. across from [　]
9. facing [　]
10. attractive [　]
11. traffic light [　]
12. be located [　]

a. 〜に面している	b. なじみがある	c. コインランドリー	d. 駐車場
e. 〜のとなり	f. 公共施設	g. 魅力的	h. 現場
i. 〜の向い側	j. 一区画	k. 〜に位置する	l. 信号

2 Complete the sentences using the vocabulary above. Change the word form (plural, etc.) if necessary.

1. City Hall and parks are some examples of _____.
2. I don't live around here, so I'm not _____ this area.
3. The shop is very close. It's on the next _____.
4. My room _____ west, so it's very hot in the afternoon.
5. The project _____ is at a very convenient location.

3 For each meaning below, write a word from 1-12 above that has the same meaning.

1. appealing; pleasing in appearance: [　　　　　]
2. place; location: [　　　　　]
3. on the other side of a street: [　　　　　]
4. a coin laundry [　　　　　]
5. the place where automobiles can be left [　　　　　]

【More Words】

path/lane ← road ← street → boulevard → avenue（street を中心に一般的に道路の規模による），one-way street 一方通行道路，two-way street 二方向道路，dead-end street 袋小路，residential 住宅の，commercial 商業の，rent out 賃貸する，bottom floor ／ ground floor 一階，appeal うける，popular 人気がある，single 独身者，include 含む，zoning regulations 区画規制，two-bedroom 2 寝室＋リビングルーム＋キッチン＋トイレ＋浴室，studio ワンルーム

PRONUNCIATION

Linked sounds

When people speak, each word is not pronounced separately. Instead, some sounds are linked together. As a result, you may not understand the words you hear even though you would have no problem reading the same words. Understanding sound linking will help you to understand what people say. It will also help you to speak more smoothly.

Consonant + Vowel（語尾の子音と次の単語の語頭の母音で 1 音のように発音します）：

Sto<u>p i</u>t. → スタッペト　　O<u>ne e</u>xample → ワニグザンプル

Di<u>d y</u>ou kno<u>w i</u>t? → ディジュノウィト？

Consonant + Consonant（同じ／とても近い子音どうしが続くときは、切らずにその音を発音する口の形を 2 音素分くらい保ちます）：

las<u>t t</u>ime → ラス・タイム

bi<u>g g</u>arage → ビグ・ガラジ

1 Paying attention to the underlined linked sounds, listen to the audio and practice the sentences.

1. Woul<u>d y</u>ou li<u>ke t</u>o start introducing the projec<u>t s</u>ite fo<u>r u</u>s?
2. seve<u>n m</u>ile<u>s s</u>outh-wes<u>t o</u>f the cente<u>r o</u>f Springfield
3. two block<u>s a</u>way from the medical clinic
4. across fro<u>m a</u> pos<u>t o</u>ffice an<u>d a</u> church
5. Tha<u>t's s</u>u<u>ch a</u> convenient location.

2 Listen to the audio and write the words you hear.

1. [　　　　　　　　　　] 2. [　　　　　　　　　　]
3. [　　　　　　　　　　] 4. [　　　　　　　　　　]
5. [　　　　　　　　　　] 6. [　　　　　　　　　　]
7. [　　　　　　　　　　] 8. [　　　　　　　　　　]

GRAMMAR POINT

Prepositions

どこに何があるか言ってみよう：**Describing locations with prepositions**（前置詞）

前置詞は、原則的に名詞の前に置かれ、主に「〜に」「〜へ」と訳されます。時、原因・理由、目的、結果、手段、材料、反対を表わすものがありますが、ここでは、現場の近隣を主なテーマとし、どこに何があるかを前置詞を使って説明できるようにしましょう。

前置詞		例
at, on, in	at：狭い場所 on: 接触している場合 in: 広い場所	at the corner of Jason and 3rd on Raymond street in America
under, above, over	under: 〜の下に above: 〜の上に over: 〜の上に（かぶさっている）	under the tree above the tree over the river
by, near, around	by: 〜のそばに near: 〜の近くに around: 〜の周りを（に）	by the river near the police station around the shopping mall
between, among	between: 2つのものの間 among: 3つ以上のものの間	between 7th and 8th street among the trees
in front of, next to/beside, across from, behind, adjacent to, facing (to), on the right, on the left など	in front of: 〜の前に next to: 〜の隣に across from: 〜の向かいに behind: 〜の後ろに adjacent to: 〜に隣接して facing (to): 〜に直面して	in front of the entrance next to/beside the drug store across from the post office behind the restaurant adjacent to the freeway

例 1

There's also a laundromat **behind** the site.

敷地の後ろにコインランドリーもあります。

例 2

There should be a green space **around** the buildings.

ビルの周りに緑化スペースがなければいけません。

1 Complete the sentences using the words in parentheses.

1. その駐車場はパイン通りに面しています。
   (The, facing, is, Pine Street, parking lot).

   _____.

2. その市役所は50世帯あるアパートの向かい側にあります。
   (City Hall, from, which, across, has, 50, is, The, apartment building, the, units).

   _____.

3. 私達のプロジェクトチームは、クライアントとウィンドランド駅で会う予定です。
   (project team, the clients, will, at, Our, meet, Windland Station).

   _____.

4. 教会の前に、沢山の木がある大きな公園があります。
   (a, is, large, There, with, park, a lot of, church, in front of, trees, the).

   _____.

5. 次の信号で右に曲がりなさい。
   (Turn, light, the, at, next, right, traffic).

   _____.

Activity (pair or small group):

Student A: Describe a place near your school by giving its location.

Student B: Guess what the place is.

   e.g. A: It's next to the post office.
   B: It's the convenience store!
   A: That's right.

Unit 2

Conversation 1

1 Practice the conversation in pairs or groups. 10

   Mika (Architect): Tom, would you like to start introducing the project site for us?
   Tom (Client): Sure, Mika. The site is in Windland, about seven miles south-west of the center of Springfield. It's at the corner of 7th Avenue and Raymond St, about a five-minute walk from Windland Station.
   Mika (Architect): Is that near the hospital?
   Tom (Client): Yes, it's about two blocks from the hospital.
   Mika (Architect): What is the address of the project site?
   Tom (Client): It's 21 Raymond Street, Windland. You can see it on the map here.
   Mika (Architect): I see. It's across from a park and a church.
   Tom (Client): Yes. The other side faces a post office, and there's a new cafe on the next corner. There's also a laundromat behind the site. It's very convenient.
   Mika (Architect): That's a great location for an apartment block.

2 Work with a partner. Fill in the blanks and make your own short conversation.

   Student A: My house is located in _____.
                It's a _____ -minute walk from _____.
   Student B: Is that near _____?
   Student A: Yes, it's about _____ blocks from _____.
   Student B: That's a great location for _____.

Activity

1. **A**: Draw a simple map from your house to the closest station in box A. Then use prepositions to give directions from your house to the station.
2. **B**: Listen to A and draw a map in box B.

A. (For student A)	B. (For student B)

17

Conversation 2

Listen to the rest of the conversation. Write all the words you can hear. Compare and discuss with your partner. 🔊 11

```
Memo
```

1 Listen to the conversation again and write T if the statement is true or F if false.
1. Tom wants to build a residential project with some commercial units. (   )
2. Tom is planning to sell the units. (   )
3. There are many stores around the site. (   )
4. The area of the project site is a popular location for young people as well. (   )
5. Mika thinks it should be all two-bedroom units in the building. (   )

2 Write answers to the questions below.
1. What type of project is Tom, the client, planning to have? [   ]
2. What number of units was Tom originally thinking of having? [   ]
3. How many two bedroom units does Mika suggest? [   ]
4. What is the total unit number Mika suggests? [   ]
5. What does Mika say the next step is? [   ]

GOOD TO KNOW

Slow City

Do you know what a slow city is? It means that the city promotes a slower life instead of a busy life that is always in a rush. The Slow Cities movement started in Italy along with slow food and slow life movements. The organization for this movement is called Cittaslow. To become an officially recognized "Slow City," towns need to pay attention to the quality of life of its residents. For example, there should be plans to create a better environment and infrastructure. There should also be efforts made to encourage local foods and production, hospitality, and a sense of community. There are many cities which have qualified as slow cities in 28 countries. In Japan, Kesennuma city and Maebashi city are among them.

Unit 3
FLOOR PLAN: Talking about rooms

OBJECTIVES

Vocabulary: To learn the names of rooms
Pronunciation: To practice word stress
Grammar: To describe the parts of a building/unit using comparatives
Conversation: To talk about building or unit amenities

Vocabulary

1 Match the words and the meanings.

1. condominium [　]
2. entrance [　]
3. balcony [　]
4. security [　]
5. amenities [　]
6. gym [　]
7. spacious [　]
8. lobby [　]
9. emergency exit [　]
10. master bedroom [　]
11. renovation [　]
12. closet [　]

a. 警備員	b. 主寝室	c. ジム	d. ベランダ
e. 玄関	f. クロゼット	g. 非常口	h. ロビー
i. 改修、改築	j. 広々とした	k. 付属施設・設備	l. 分譲マンション

2 Complete the sentences using the vocabulary above. Change the word form (plural, etc.) if necessary.

1. A sauna and pool are nice _____ to have.
2. A _____ is a nice facility to have so that people can exercise there.
3. The _____ is the largest of the three bedrooms.
4. The door of an _____ should always be able to open from the inside.
5. The _____ of this unit is large and nice for relaxing outside.

3 For each meaning below, write a word from 1 to 12 above that has the same meaning.

1. the process of repairing and improving a building [　　　　]
2. an entrance hall of a building, usually with a large space [　　　　]
3. a space or a smaller room where you can keep clothing and other things [　　　　]
4. a residential building in which the units are owned by individuals [　　　　]
5. a system to keep a place safe [　　　　]

19

【More Words】

theater room シアタールーム, meeting room 会議室, walkway 通路, locker ロッカー, closet クロゼット, walk-in closet ウォークインクロゼット, front yard 前庭, back yard 裏庭, studio =ワンルーム+キッチン+バスルーム 1-bedroom and 1-bath =１寝室+リビングルーム+キッチン+バスルーム, 2-bedroom and 1 ½-bath (one and a half-bath) =2寝室+リビングルーム+キッチン+バスルーム+シャワールーム, sauna サウナ, exercise 運動, BBQ facilities バーベキュー設備, grill グリル, reduce 減らす, 15 m x 5 m (15 meters by 5 meters), particular 特別の, downstairs 階下（の）, storage 収納・倉庫

PRONUNCIATION

Word Stress

Native speakers do not pronounce every single word with equal strength. Words that carry important information, called *content words*, are pronounced strongly and clearly. On the other hand, *function words* like articles, prepositions, or pronouns are pronounced weakly. Use a mixture of strong and weak stress to improve your English rhythm and make your English easier to understand.

1 Underline the words that carry important information. Listen to the CD and check which words are pronounced strongly/clearly. Then practice reading the sentences with the CD.

a. A sauna and pool are attractive amenities to have in an apartment building.

b. A gym is a useful amenity to have because people can exercise without going out.

c. Among the bedrooms, a master bedroom is usually the largest.

d. The door of an emergency exit should always be able to open from the inside.

e. The balcony of this unit is large. It will fit a good size table and chairs.

GRAMMAR POINT

Comparatives

部屋・建物・地域を比べてみよう：Comparing rooms/building/areas using *comparatives*（比較級）

比較には原級・比較級・最上級と3つありましたね。ここでは、比べるものを他の部屋、建物、地域と限定して、これらを比較するときに便利な表現「～と同じくらい…」、「～ほど…ない」、そして「～の何倍…」を復習しましょう。

- 「～と同じくらい…」as 原級 as~

    The lobby of this condominium is **as beautiful as** the one in City Hall.
    The amenities of this building are **as nice as** the ones of that building.

- 「～ほど…ない」not as 原級 as~

    The other two bedrooms are **not as large as** the master bedroom.
    The balcony of this unit **is not as spacious as** the one of that unit.

- 「～の何倍…」twice/three times/half as~as

    Their garden with BBQ facilities is **twice as large as** our garden.
    The lobby with security desks is **three times as spacious as** the lobby without one.

1 Complete the sentences using the words in parentheses.

1. 一般的に、後庭は前庭ほど大きくありません。

    (Generally, the, front, speaking, not, large, backyard, is, as, as, the, yard).

    _____.

2. 主寝室は他の寝室の2倍の大きさです。

    (The, the other rooms, master, is, twice, as, bedroom, as, big).

    _____.

3. マンションのプールは公共体育館のと同じくらい長いです。

    (The, pool, as, at, our, is, long, public, as, the, one, at, condominium, the, gym).

    _____.

4. 私達の部屋のベランダは隣の部屋のベランダよりも大きいです。

    (The balcony, than, of, the one, our unit, is, larger, of, next unit).

    _____.

5. この建物のこちら側は、反対側ほど騒がしくない。

    (This side, as, noisy, of, the building, is, not, as, the other side).

    _____.

Conversation 1

1 Practice the conversation in pairs or groups.

3 Bedroom / 2.5 Bath
2200 S.F.

Mika (Architect): Tom, let me hear your ideas on amenities for the building.
Tom (Client): Well, it'd be nice to have a garden with BBQ facilities, a gym, and a pool.
Mika: What do you think, Cindy?
Cindy (landscape engineer): These are all possible. The gym should be inside the building. I'd suggest a pool in the garden that's 15 m x 5 m in size and has 4 BBQ grills with tables.
Tom: Can the pool be a little bigger than that?
Cindy: That depends. If we can reduce the number of tables, the pool can be bigger. Would fewer BBQs be OK?
Tom: OK. Two will be enough then.
Mika: If there are two BBQ grills with tables, how big can the pool be?
Cindy: Well, it can be a little longer but not much wider: 20 meters would be the maximum.
Tom: That'll be fine.
Mika: Are there any particular amenities that you want for the units?
Tom: Yes. I want all of the units to have a spacious balcony. I also want each one to have good storage. Also, downstairs there should be a lobby with a security desk and sofas.
Mika: Sure. All of these are possible. Stan and Ed will be here in a moment. We can start discussing the kitchen and bathroom when they arrive.

2 Work with a partner. Fill in the blanks and make your own short conversation.

Student A: _____, let me hear your ideas on amenities for the building.
Student B: Well, I'd like to have _____ in the garden.
Student A: Are there any particular amenities you want for the units?
Student B: Yes. I want _____ in each unit. What do you think?
Student A: Well, I think that _____.

Unit 3

Conversation 2

Listen to the rest of the conversation. Write all the words you can hear. Compare and discuss with your partner. 🎧 15

```
Memo



```

1 Listen to the conversation again and write T if the statement is true or F if false.
1. Tom wants the penthouse units to be larger than the units on other floors. (   )
2. Tom wants to have two bathrooms for the top floor units. (   )
3. Tom's daughter has two children now. (   )
4. Mika thinks it's a good idea to have larger units on the top floor. (   )
5. Tom and his wife are going to live in one of the penthouse units permanently. (   )

2 Listen to the conversation again and fill in the blanks below.
1. Tom wants to talk about the possibility of penthouse units before going into the details of the _____.
2. Tom wants the larger units to have more _____.
3. Tom wants the penthouse unit to have _____ bedrooms.
4. The master bedroom should be the _____ of the bedrooms.
5. Tom and his wife are going to live in one penthouse unit, and _____ in the other.

Activity (pair or small group):

In the story above, Tom is building an apartment building which includes an apartment for his daughter. Imagine you are building your own dream house or apartment.

Take out a piece of paper.
① Take two minutes to draw/write your ideas.
② Talk about your dream home to your partner/group members.
③ Compare your dream house/apartment with those of other members using as many comparatives sentences as possible.

GOOD TO KNOW
Half a room? Three-quarter bath?

Different countries have different ways of counting rooms in a unit/house. In Switzerland, rooms that are rather small, are not always considered to be a whole room. A very small room, such as the entrance, a walk in closet, or even a kitchen is often indicated as a half room. In America, you often see house sizes like 4 bedrooms and 2 ½ (two and a half) bathrooms. In general, a full bathroom consists of a bathtub, a shower, a toilet, and a sink. A ¾ (three quarters) bathroom consists of a shower, a toilet, and a vanity sink. ½ (a half) bathroom means that there is only a toilet and a sink.

Unit 4
BUILDING STRUCTURE: Talking about building structure and materials

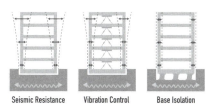

OBJECTIVES

Vocabulary: To learn words related to building structure
Pronunciation: To practice the pronunciation of /ər/ and /ɑr/
Grammar: To describe building structures using quantifiers
Conversation: To talk about building materials and structure

Vocabulary

1 Match the words and the meanings.

1. horizontal [ ]
2. vertical [ ]
3. reinforced concrete [ ]
4. steel structure [ ]
5. grid [ ]
6. five-story building [ ]
7. expect [ ]
8. formwork [ ]
9. wood structure [ ]
10. insert [ ]
11. pour [ ]
12. made out of [ ]

a. 垂直の	b. 水平の	c. 期待する	d. 鋼構造
e. グリッド、(鉄)格子	f. 5階建ての建物	g. 鉄筋コンクリート	h. 型枠
i. 木造	j. 挿入する	k. 注ぎいれる	l. ～からできている

2 Complete the sentences using vocabulary above. Change the word form (plural, etc.) if necessary.

1. Draw a _____ line from left to right.
2. Please _____ your credit card into the machine.
3. We will _____ the concrete into the mold.
4. This toy is _____ soft rubber.
5. Reinforced concrete is concrete that is reinforced with a steel _____.

【More Words】

steel bars 鋼棒, assemble 組み立てる, horizontally 水平に, vertically 垂直に, suitable 適切な, materials 材料, practical 実用的な, completely 完全に, atmosphere 雰囲気, whole picture 全体像, basement 地下, foundations 基礎, frame 骨組, finishing 仕上げ, stylish 恰好の良い, common area 共有部, precast concrete プレキャストコンクリート, cast-in-place concrete 場所打ちコンクリート, brick 煉瓦, concrete block コンクリートブロック, glass block ガラスブロック, timber ／ lumber 木材, dwelling part 住居部分

PRONUNCIATION

/ər/ or /ar/?

It is very difficult to hear the difference between these two sounds. For /ər/ you keep your mouth very slightly open, while for /ar/ your chin goes way down. You may hear a long /ə/ and /a/ without an /r/ sound in British English.

1 Listen and practice the words below.

1. /ər/   exp<u>er</u>t   c<u>ur</u>ve   t<u>er</u>mite   w<u>or</u>d   elevat<u>or</u>
2. /ar/   <u>ar</u>chitect   f<u>ar</u>m   h<u>ear</u>t   h<u>ar</u>d   st<u>ar</u>

2 Listen to the CD and circle the word you hear in each pair of words.

1. stir（かき混ぜる）/ star（星）
2. curve（カーブ）/ carve（切る、彫る）
3. hurt（痛む、傷つける）/ heart（心、心臓）
4. firm（会社）/ farm（農場）
5. word（言葉）/ ward（棟、区）

GRAMMAR POINT

Quantifiers

建物の構造に関する度合や程度を表現してみよう：**Describing things using quantifiers**（数量詞）
数量詞は、名詞の前に置かれます。ニュアンスが少しずつ違うので注意が必要です。
ここでは、建物の構造に関する基本的な数量詞を復習しましょう。

● 可算名詞 (many, few) か不可算名詞 (much, little) かで異なる数量詞

The project team will have **many** chances to discuss the structure of building.

They didn't have **much** time to examine the materials being used in the building.

Unit 4

● 「ほとんど～」と訳される数量詞

	品詞	注意
almost	副詞	動詞、形容詞、副詞を修飾する 「もう少しのところでその状態になっていない」のニュアンス
most	形容詞 代名詞	形容詞：most 名詞 代名詞：most of the 名詞
nearly	副詞	動詞、形容詞、副詞を修飾する 否定後の前に置く事はできない。
mostly	副詞	動詞、形容詞、副詞を修飾する 「その大半がその状態であるという」のニュアンス

1 Complete the sentences using the words in the parentheses.

1. この周辺のほとんどすべての建物はコンクリートでできている。
   (Almost, of, are, buildings, made, all, this area, concrete, the, of, in).

   _____.

2. 建物の骨組みはほとんど組み立てられた。
   (The frame, building, has, assembled, mostly, been, of, the).

   _____.

3. 私達は、そのプロジェクトのほとんどの計画を話し合った。
   (We, for, have, the plans, discussed, most of, the project).

   _____.

4. そのプロジェクトはほとんど完成した。
   (The, nearly, is, completed, project).

   _____.

5. 1995年の南部地震でダメージを受けた建物の多くは当時の建築基準を満たしていた。
   (Many, in the 1995 Nambu Earthquake, satisfied, damaged buildings, the existing regulations).

   _____.

Conversation 1

1 Practice the conversation in pairs or groups. 19

    Tom: Can you tell me more about the plans for the project?
    Mika: Of course. Well, to begin with, it will be built out of reinforced concrete.
    Tom: Concrete? Is there a reason for it being concrete? I expected it to be a wooden structure.
    Mika: Oh really? Most residential buildings of this size are built using reinforced concrete.
    Tom: What is reinforced concrete? I know concrete, but what does reinforced mean?
    Mika: It means that the concrete is made stronger by having steel bars inside it.
    Tom: How do you put the steel into the concrete?
    Brian: First, steel bars placed both vertically and horizontally are connected to each other as a grid. Next, wooden boards, we call them formwork, are assembled around the steel bars. Then mixed concrete is poured into the formwork. Once the concrete gets hard enough, the formwork will be removed.
    Tom: I see. So the idea is to make the building strong by combining steel and concrete.
    Brian: Yes. That's right.
    Tom: Do you have enough space to make it all?
    Brian: Some of the reinforced concrete will be brought directly from the factory. There won't be any problem with space to make it.

2 Work with a partner. For 1. fill in the blanks using the conversation above. For 2. work together using your own ideas. Share with your classmates.

1. **Student A**: The process of making reinforced concreted is ….
   Student B: First, _____.
                   Then _____.
   Student A: Yes, and _____ after that.

2. **Student B**: The process of making _____ is ….
   Student A: First, _____.
                   Then _____.
   Student B: Yes, and _____ after that.

Conversation 2

Listen to the rest of the conversation. Write all the words you can hear. Compare and discuss with your partner. 🆑 20

Memo

1 Listen to the conversation again and write T if the statement is true or F if false.
1. Concrete structures are always made at the site. (   )
2. Precast concrete is not good for residential buildings. (   )
3. Tom wanted a wooden look to the building. (   )
4. Tom likes the idea of wooden decking on the common amenity area. (   )
5. Mika disagrees with the idea of using wood in the common area. (   )

2 Listen to the conversation again and fill in the blanks below.
1. Tom now has a _____ of suitable building materials.
2. Tom didn't know that concrete parts could be made at _____.
3. Precast concrete is useful for construction sites without _____.
4. Although the structure is reinforced concrete, the _____ can still be wood.
5. Tom thinks that the wooden decking would create a _____ atmosphere.

GOOD TO KNOW

Structural Regulations

In Japan, structural regulations for buildings began to be introduced in 1924 after the Kanto Earthquake. It was the first time that seismic force was defined in the regulations. The Building Standard Law was enacted in 1950 and some regulations were revised 1971 and 1981. Even if buildings satisfy the structural regulations, they may suffer heavy damage when severe earthquakes occur. Most of the buildings which were severely damaged in the 1995 Great Hanshin-Awaji Earthquake satisfied structural regulations of the time of construction but did not satisfy the latest regulations. However, severe damage was observed even among some buildings which satisfied the regulations at the time. Therefore, some regulations were revised after the earthquake.

Unit 5
KITCHEN: Talking about kitchen design and appliances

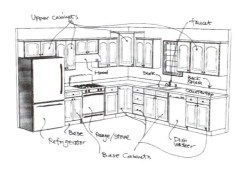

OBJECTIVES

Vocabulary: To learn words for describing kitchens
Pronunciation: To practice consonant clusters
Grammar: To give opinions about the kitchen using conjunctions
Conversation: To talk about kitchen layout and basic kitchen appliances

Vocabulary

1 Match the words and the meanings.

1. appliance [　]
2. refrigerator [　]
3. stove/range [　]
4. cooktop [　]
5. dishwasher [　]
6. exhaust fan [　]
7. garbage disposal unit [　]
8. cupboard [　]
9. microwave oven [　]
10. faucet [　]
11. freezer [　]
12. storage [　]

a. 蛇口	b. 調理台	c. 食器棚	d. 生ごみ処理機
e. 食洗機	f. 冷蔵庫	g. 電子レンジ	h. 電化製品
i. レンジ	j. 換気扇	k. 冷凍庫	l. 倉庫

2 Complete the sentences using the vocabulary above. Change the word form (plural, etc.) if necessary.

1. I want to buy a _____ that has a large freezer.
2. You can find all kinds of _____ in Akihabara.
3. The _____ has to have enough storage space for food and dishes.
4. This _____ also has a toaster function.
5. Water is dripping from the _____. We need to call a plumber.
6. Is the _____ powerful enough to remove smoke and food smells?

【More Words】

 21

open kitchen 対面式キッチン，closed kitchen 独立型キッチン，furnished 家具付き，partly furnished 一部家具付き，spacious ゆったりした，pre-installed 作り付けされた，pantry 食品庫，it's up to ~ それは~次第，tenant 借家人／居住者，functional 機能的な，appliance 什器（じゅうき：家具・食器・電化製品などの日常生活で使用する道具類）

31

PRONUNCIATION

Consonant Clusters

Many English words have two or more consonants in sequence such an "ap**pl**iance." Also many English words end with consonant(s) such as "furni**sh**." Japanese people tend to insert a vowel between consonants. It is because Japanese syllables are always either a vowel or a combination of a consonant and a vowel.

Consonant (C), Vowel (V)

exhaust (VCCVCC)	/ɪgzɔ́ːst/	Not /ɪgzɔ́ːstʊ/
cupboard (CVCVC)	/kʌ́bɚd/	Not /kʌ́bɚdʊ/
appliance (VCCVVC)	/əpláɪəns/	Not /əpláɪənsʊ/

1 Write the following katakana-English in correct English. Listen to the CD and compare the pronunciation in katakana and in English. 🎧 22

1. レンジ [　　　　] 2. エルシェイプキッチン [　　　　]
3. テナント [　　　　] 4. カップボード [　　　　]
5. パントリー [　　　　] 6. インストール [　　　　]

GRAMMAR POINT

Conjunction

キッチンについての意見・考えを言ってみよう：Giving opinions about kitchens using *conjunctions*（接続詞）

沢山の接続詞がありますが、ここでは、but と and、特に so と not only A but also B に焦点をあて、復習しましょう。これらの接続詞を使用して単語や節などをつなげ、キッチンのレイアウトやキッチンにある電化製品について意見を言ってみましょう。

● but「〜しかし ...」

I can give some suggestions for the faucets, **but** I will let Tom choose.

● and「〜と ...」

The cupboards need to have enough storage space for food **and** dishes.
Does Tom want the kitchen **and** living room furnished?

● so「だから、それで、したがって」

We installed an exhaust fan above the range, **so** we will not have a problem with smoke and food smells.
→ so の直前にコンマを置きます。

There are too many kinds of faucets, **so** I cannot make a decision.
→ so の後には主語 + 動詞 （節）を置きます。

The L-shaped kitchen leaves more space for the living room, **so** I would prefer an L-shape.

● Not only A but also B「A だけでなく B も ...」

This huge exhaust fan removes **not only** smoke **but also** food smells.
→ A と B は同じ種類の語にします。

The cupboard is big enough to store **not only** food **but** dishes.
→ also は省略される場合があります。
When you decide the kitchen design, you need to think about **not only** design **but also** how easy it is to use.
→ 動詞の形は B に合わせます。

1 Complete the sentences using the words in the parentheses.

1. U 字型のキッチンは収納庫や作業スペースがより多くある。
   (U-shaped kitchens, work space, provide, storage, more, and).

   _____.

2. キッチンにあるディスポーザ（生ゴミ粉砕処理システム）は便利なので、取り付けたい。
   (A, in, the kitchen, garbage disposal unit, is, one, useful, so, I, to, would like, install).

   _____.

3. L 字型のキッチンはダイニングだけでなく、リビングもより広くする。
   (An, larger, L-shaped kitchen, not, makes, dining, only, the, but, also, the, living space).

   _____.

4. 家の食品庫は機能的で広いので気に入っている。
   (I, and, like, the pantry, because, in my house, it, functional, is, spacious).

   _____.

Conversation 1

1 Practice the conversation in pairs or groups. 23

Stan: Mika, this is the kitchen layout. You said Tom was planning to have all units partly furnished. Is that right?
Mika: Yes, that's right.
Stan: What appliances does he want?
Mika: He wants the basic appliances; a refrigerator and a range for the kitchen.
Stan: I have included a dishwasher, too. Is that OK?
Mika: Yes. That's perfect. A dishwasher is not only useful for the tenants but it will also make the units easier to rent. Are you planning to have a single or double sink?
Stan: Either way is fine. It's up to Tom.
Mika: OK. I'll suggest a double sink to him. Are you installing a garbage disposal unit?
Stan: Yes, it reduces the amount of garbage that needs to be put out.
Mika: All right. I'll show Tom this layout plan.
Stan: If Tom doesn't like the L-shaped kitchen as I drew it, let me know. I can change it to an island kitchen or U-shaped kitchen.
Mika: Sure. Thanks.

2 Practice the conversation on page 33 in pairs. Then, using the words in the box, complete and practice the conversation below.

rice cooker 炊飯器	toaster トースター	dishwasher 食洗機
garbage disposal unit 生ごみ処理機	fridge (refrigerator) 冷蔵庫	microwave 電子レンジ
coffee machine コーヒーメーカー	water purifier 浄水器	washing machine 洗濯機
vacuum cleaner 掃除機	humidifier 加湿器	hair dryer ドライヤー
air conditioner エアコン		

1. A: What appliances do you have at home?
   B: I have _____ and _____.
   A: Are there any other appliances you want?
   B: I want _____ because _____.

2. A: What three appliances do you think are the most or least important to have in an apartment unit?
   B: I think _____, _____, and _____ are important but not _____.

3 Work with a partner.
① Student A and B: Draw a kitchen layout.
② Student A: Describe your kitchen layout to Student B. Student B: Listen and draw the layout.
③ Take turns and repeat.
④ Check if the layout you have drawn matches your partner's description.

A.	B.

Activity (Pair work)

Read the descriptions of kitchen types below. Write the name of the kitchen type in each [ ] and share with your partner. If you disagree with your partner's answers, explain why.

1. It takes up only one stretch of wall space. For small homes, it's a good layout.
   [   ]
2. More people can work at the same time without bumping into each other.
   [   ]

3. With two separate counters in parallel on both sides, you can wash vegetables and cook by simply turning around. [   ]
4. The work-flow line is open on both sides and is easy to come and go.
   [   ]
5. This kitchen has a work space on three sides, which provides a lot of counter space, even in a small area. [   ]
6. This kitchen has a work space on four sides. There is a lot of space for counters and cupboards. [   ]

L-SHAPED KITCHEN	U-SHAPED KITCHEN	ISLAND KITCHEN
IN-LINE KITCHEN	GALLEY KITCHEN	G-SHAPED KITCHEN

Conversation 2

Listen to the rest of the conversation. Write all the words you can hear. Compare and discuss with your partner.. 24

Memo

1 Listen to the conversation again and write T if the statement is true or F if false.

1. Mika is showing Tom the kitchen layout she made. (   )
2. The refrigerator is at one end of the layout. (   )
3. Mika thinks that a microwave oven should be included in the base kitchen appliances. (   )
4. There is a pantry in the kitchen. (   )

2 Listen to the conversation again and write the answers to the questions below.

1. What type of kitchen is Mika describing to Tom?
   _____.

2. Was a dishwasher included in Stan's original kitchen layout?
   _____.

3. What is the space above the stove going to be?
   _____.

4. Where is the pantry going to be placed?
   _____.

GOOD TO KNOW

Yes or No?

When a question is in a negative or tag question, you may be unsure about how to answer. Read the sentences below to learn how to respond.

1. Don't you want to install a garbage disposal unit?
   Yes, I do (want to install one). / No, I don't (want to install one).

2. Can't Tom choose the faucets?
   Yes, he can (choose them). / No, he can't (choose them).

3. You are installing a garbage disposal unit, aren't you?
   Yes, I am (installing one). / No, I am not (installing one).

4. Would you mind if I open the window?
   Yes, (I would mind). = I don't want you to open it. /
   No, (I wouldn't mind). = It's OK for you to open it.

Unit 6
DINING & LIVING ROOM: Talking about furniture

OBJECTIVES

Vocabulary: To learn various kinds of furniture
Pronunciation: To practice the diphthongs /aɪ, aʊ, ɪe, ɔɪ, oʊ/
Grammar: To describe living and dining rooms using gerunds and infinitives
Conversation: To talk about arranging furniture in the living room

Vocabulary

1 Match the words and the meanings.

1. unit layout [ ]
2. penthouse [ ]
3. couch [ ]
4. recliner [ ]
5. loveseat [ ]
6. potted plants [ ]
7. sketch [ ]
8. item [ ]
9. arrange [ ]
10. shelf [ ]
11. TV stand [ ]
12. comfort [ ]

a. 配置する   b. ペントハウス   c. 快適さ   d. リクライナー
e. ユニットレイアウト   f. 鉢植え植物   g. 二人掛けソファ   h. 三人掛けソファ
i. スケッチ   j. 物   k. 棚   l. テレビ台

2 Complete the sentences using vocabulary above. Change the word form (plural, etc.) if necessary.

1. My room is small, so a loveseat would be better than a _____.
2. A _____ unit of a condominium is usually more expensive than the units on other floors.
3. An interior designer makes a _____ of the unit-layout and shows it to a client.
4. A _____ can change the angle of the chairback for your comfort.
5. You shouldn't put too many _____ in one room.

【More Words】 25

cabinet キャビネット，influential 影響力のある，compact コンパクト，place 置く、設置する，basically 基本的に，arrangement 配置，regret 後悔する，bookshelf 本棚，coffee table コーヒーテーブル，rocking chair ロッキングチェア，magazine rack マガジンラック，beanbag chair ビーンバッグチェア，hammock ハンモック，ottoman オットマン、足乗せ用ソファー， end table エンドテーブル（ソファの隣など置く小卓），coat rack コート掛け

PRONUNCIATION

Diphthongs

The combination of two vowels in a single syllable such, as /aɪ/ in *price*, /aʊ/ in *couch*, /eɪ/ in *layout*, /ɔɪ/ in *choice*, and /oʊ/ in *rope is* known as a dipthong. Among these diphthongs, Japanese people tend to pronounce /eɪ/ and /oʊ/ as one long vowel like /e:/ and /o:/ in some katakana-words (loan words). The meanings can usually be understood from context, but there are some cases which may cause confusion, such as *boat/bought* and *coat/caught*.

1 Listen to the CD and practice pronouncing words with diphthongs.

1. レーアウト → layout /léɪaʊt/
2. ステーション → station /stéɪʃən/
3. コート → coat /kóʊt/
4. ボート → boat /bóʊt/
5. デート → date /déɪt/
6. スペース → space /spéɪs/

2 Work with a partner and list up some more katakana words (loan words) that use long vowels like the examples above.

_____ _____ _____ _____

GRAMMAR POINT

Gerund and Infinitive

動名詞／To 不定詞を使って、リビング・ダイニングルームについて話してみよう：Talking about living/dining rooms using *gerund*（動名詞）or *infinitive*（不定詞）forms

目的語に動名詞・不定詞が取れるかは動詞によって異なります。また、目的語に両方取れますが、意味が変わる表現がありので、紛らわしいですね。ここでは、リビングやダイニングルームによく置いてある家具やリビングやダイニングのレイアウトに関連つけ、以上の2点に注意しながら復習していきましょう。

● 目的語に不定詞を取る動詞：agree, decide, hope, learn, need, refuse など
  She **decided not to** have a recliner in her living room.
  The young family doesn't **need to** have too many pieces of furniture.

● 目的語に動名詞を取る動詞：admit, enjoy, appreciate, finish, practice など
  Sherry **advises having** potted plants will make the room more relaxing.
  Sherry **suggests placing** some more plants in the living room.

● 意味が変わる表現：remember, forget, try, regret, stop など
  remember to do：〜することを覚えている（未来のニュアンス）
  remember 〜ing：〜したことを覚えている（過去のニュアンス）

  Please **remember to** place the book on the bookshelf when you have finished reading it.
  （読み終えたら本を本棚に戻すことを覚えていてください）
  I **remember** plac**ing** the book on the bookshelf but I cannot find it.
  （本棚に本を戻したことを覚えていますが、その本が見つかりません）

Unit 6

1 Choose the appropriate expression in parentheses below.

1. Sherry suggests (to have, having) a rocking chair and a magazine rack in the living room.

2. The living room for the young family needs (being, to be) spacious for young children.

3. Please excuse my (interrupting, to interrupt) you while you're having your dinner.

4. Tom asked Sherry (to put, putting) a recliner in the living room.

5. Tom wants (installing, to install) a good size bookshelf in the living room.

2 Complete the sentences using the words in the parentheses.

1. トムはどんな色のソファがほしいかミカに伝えるのを忘れた。
   (Tom, tell, forgot to, the color, for, Mika, he, wants, the sofa).

   _____.

2. 彼女はキッチンに置く植物を買うために立ち止まった。
   (She, for, some potted plants, stopped to, buy, the kitchen).

   _____.

3. 私たちはその部屋に欲しい家具のリストを作り終わった。
   (We, in the room, the list of furniture, finished, we want, making).

   _____.

Activity (pair or small group)

Think about a reason and complete each sentence below. Write a clause (having a subject and a verb) after *because*.

1. I want to have a large coffee table because _____
   _____.

2. A bookshelf is a must-have item because _____
   _____.

3. I'd like open space in the living room because _____
   _____.

4. I'd like some plants in the living room because _____
   _____.

5. I need to have a sofa because _____
   _____.

Conversation 1

1 Practice the conversation in pairs or groups. 27

Sherry: I got the unit layout of the penthouse from Mika this morning. Now, I am thinking about how to arrange the furniture.
Tom: Oh, thanks.
Sherry: Could you tell me what kind of furniture you're thinking of having?
Tom: Well, I want the living room to be as relaxing as possible, so there should be a couch. I enjoy reading, so a recliner would be a comfortable place to sit.
Sherry: You mentioned that you also want bookshelves, a TV stand, and a coffee table. Is there anything else?
Tom: Oh, I want to have a loveseat as well.
Sherry: All right. I think it's better to have some potted plants, too. It'll give the room a fresh feeling.
Tom: Oh yes. I'd like to have some plants in the living room.
Sherry: OK. How about the other unit on the top floor for your daughter's family?
Tom: I've talked to her, and she said she wants basically the same items as my unit except the recliner. She would rather have more open space in the living room.
Sherry: Of course. It's always nice to have open space for young children to run around.

2 Complete the short conversation and practice with your partner.

Student A: What kinds of furniture do you want to have in the living room?
Student B: Well. I need to have _____.
Student A: Is there anything else?
Student B: It would be nice to have _____.
Student A: Well, I think you shouldn't have _____.
Student B: Why is that?
Student A: It's because _____.

Conversation 2

Listen to the rest of the conversation. Write all the words you can hear. Compare and discuss with your partner. 🎧 28

> **Memo**

1 Listen to the conversation again and write T if the statement is true or F if false.
1. Tom is showing Sherry a sketch he made. (   )
2. Tom and Sherry are talking about the master bedroom. (   )
3. Tom wants to change the location of the television. (   )
4. Tom is satisfied with the location of the couch. (   )
5. Tom suggests a change to Sherry. (   )

2 Listen to the conversation again and write the answers to the questions below.
1. What is Sherry showing Tom? _____
2. What has Sherry placed in front of the window? _____
3. What will be facing the couch? _____
4. What will be between the couch and the loveseat? _____
5. Where does Tom want to put a bookshelf? _____

Activity (pair or small group)

① Draw a living room with your arrangement of furniture in Box A. Place at least five items of furniture in your room.
② Describe your furniture arrangement to your partner
③ Listen to your partner and draw what you hear in box B
④ Check if your partner' drawing is the same as yours.

A	B

GOOD TO KNOW

Architects are not only designing buildings

Some architects design furniture as well. This is because in architecture it is important to design the whole space. For example, Le Corbusier, the influential Swiss born French architect, designed furniture including a series of chairs and tables. He designed LC1(see picture), LC2, and LC4 in 1928. Antoni Gaudi is also known as an architect who designed furniture. Gaudi made wooden benches decorated with carved flowers on the back.

(Le Corbusier LC1)

Unit 7
DESIGN & STYLE: Talking about windows and lighting

OBJECTIVES

Vocabulary: To learn different types of windows
Pronunciation: To practice /l/ at the end of a word
Grammar: To describe the living room using adjectives and adverbs a living room
Conversation: To talk about different window types in an apartment

Vocabulary

1 Match the words and the meanings.

1. suggestions [ ]   2. vary [ ]   3. install [ ]
4. confusing [ ]   5. suitable [ ]   6. hinge [ ]
7. outward [ ]   8. depend on [ ] 9. insects [ ]
10. flow [ ]   11. security [ ] 12. allow [ ]

a. 外側へ	b. 流れ	c. 蝶番	d. 昆虫
e. ~を可能にする	f. ~によって	g. 安全	h. 異なる
i. 提案	j. 最適な	k. わかりにくい	l. 設置する

2 Complete the sentences using the vocabulary above. Change the word form (plural, etc.) if necessary.

1. His explanation is _____. I don't understand what he is trying to say.
2. I don't like any _____: the worst is cockroaches!
3. Social customs _____ greatly from country to country.
4. Please give me your _____. I can't decide what kind of window is suitable here.
5. Having windows on both sides of the room _____ the air to flow through the room.

43

3 For each meaning below, write a word from 1-12 on page 43 that has the same meaning.

1. A movable joint on a door, gate, or window: [   ]
2. To put (equipment or machinery) in position or make it ready for use: [   ]
3. Protection from danger, risk, etc.: [   ]
4. A smooth movement of air, water, people, etc.: [   ]
5. Towards the outside [   ]

【More Words】 29

screens 網戸，consume 消費する，airy 風通しの良い，messy 散らかっている，amaze 驚く，hardly ~ ほとんど～しない，available 入手できる，electrical wiring 電気配線，makes sense それは言えてる，downlights 天井はめ込みスポットライト，ceiling fan 天井ファン，cozy こじんまりして居心地の良い，focal point 焦点，purpose 目的，track 窓のレール，ideal 理想的，awning window 突き出し窓、オーニング窓，sliding windows 引違い窓，double-hung windows 上げ下げ窓

PRONUNCIATION

/l/ at the end of a word

Japanese people tend to think /r/ is a difficult sound to make, and that /r/ and /l/ are hard to distinguish. You don't have to worry too much about /r/ and /l/ because the meanings you wish to make are usually understandable from context. When you say "You are right," people won't misunderstand it with "You are light." However, words ending with /l/ may cause some difficulty for you, even with very basic and familiar words like *call*.

To make a final /l/ sound, place the tip of your tongue on your alveolar ridge (hard area behind your top front teeth) while you produce the sound /l/ and hold it there longer than you think natural. Be careful not to add /u/ like the katakana「ル」.

1 Listen to the CD and practice pronouncing the following words. 30

1. apple   2. possible   3. still
4. arrival   5. hotel   6. special

2 Listen to the CD and write the words you hear. 31

1. [   ]   2. [   ]   3. [   ]
4. [   ]   5. [   ]   6. [   ]

GRAMMAR POINT

Adjectives and Adverbs

部屋の状況などを表してみよう：**Describing rooms with adjectives**（形容詞）**and adverbs**（副詞）

皆さんは「あの映画は面白かった！」をどのように言いますか？ "That movie was interested / interesting." どちらを使いますか？また、"I am bored." を "I am boring." と間違えやすいですね。ここでは、これらのややこしい用法と部屋の状況を表すときに便利な形容詞と副詞をいくつか復習しましょう。

- **many と much の用法**

    (×) There are **many** furniture in this living room.

    (○) There is **much/a lot of** furniture in this living room.

    many は数を表す場合に使用されるので、不可算名詞には使えません。

    この場合、furniture は不可算名詞なので、much か a lot of を使用します。

    I sweep the floor in my living room **many** times a day.

    この場合、time は回数を表しているので、可算名詞になり、many を使用します。

    I don't have **much** time to clean my children's messy rooms.

    この場合、time は時間（量）を表しているので、much を使用します。

- **間違えやすい「形容詞～ ed、～ ing」**

    The view from the living room is **amazing**.

    The guests were **amazed** by the view from the living room.

    基本的には ~ed は、人の感情を説明に使い、~ing は物事の説明に使います。

    間違える人の多いものに、be interesing/interested, be boring/bored, be surprising/surprised 等々があります。

- **「多い・少ない」「高い・安い」で間違いやすい形容詞**

    The price of the penthouse units is very **high** （○）.

    The price of the penthouse units is very **expensive** （×）.

1 Choose the appropriate word.

1. Having many types of windows sounds a bit (confusing, confused).
2. This is such a (small, narrow) bathroom.
3. The architect tried (hard, hardly) to explain the different types of bedrooms.
4. There are (many, much) different kinds of windows available.

2 Complete the sentences using the words in parentheses.

1. ミカは、窓の特徴について簡潔に説明しようと一生懸命試みた。
   (Mika, to explain, tried hard, simply, the features of windows).

   _____.

2. 友人は私の散らかった部屋を見て驚いた。
   (My, messy room, friend, was, to, surprised, see, my).

   _____.

3. 普通の窓の価格は、比較的安いです。
   (The, price, relatively, of, regular windows, is, low).

   _____.

4. シェリーは、何回計画を修正しましたか？
   (How, many, revised, times, has, Sherry, the plans)?

   _____?

Conversation 1

1 Practice the conversation in pairs or groups.   32

Mika: Sherry will explain to you her suggestions for the windows.

Tom: OK. I haven't thought about windows much. Are there many different types?

Mika: Yes. The type varies depending on the location in the apartment and the purpose.

Tom: OK. The sketch says an awning window in the bathroom. What's that?

Sherry: It's a window that has a hinge on the top and opens outward. It's ideal for bathrooms. It will allow the air to flow through but is still good for security and privacy.

Tom: I see. That's good. Sliding windows? They're just regular windows that slide left or right along a track? Is that right?

Sherry: Yes. You can also see here on the plans that I'm thinking of putting double-hung windows in the bedroom. These windows slide up and down, so you can open either the bottom or the top.

Tom: Oh, I see. It's better for privacy than sliding windows.

Sherry: That's right. You get a lot of light and air, but people can't see in.

Tom: I'd like to have screens on the windows too.

Sherry: Sure. We can add that.

Unit 7

2 Match the drawings of different windows and the explanations below.

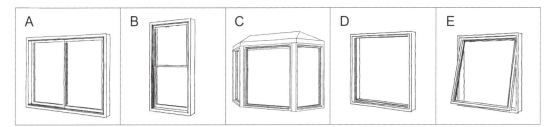

1. You may choose *a fixed window* when you need light but you don't want to open it. [ ]
2. *A double-hung window* opens by sliding up or down. Either the bottom or the top half of the window opens. [ ]
3. *A sliding window* opens by sliding left to right. [ ]
4. *An awning window* has a hinge at the top and opens outward. [ ]
5. *A bay window* allows in more light and has space to put plants or decorations. [ ]

Activity

Talk about the different windows illustrated above with your partner.
1. Explain what kind of window it is. (e.g. An awning window is a window that …)
2. Explain what is the advantage of this kind of window (e.g. This window is good for getting natural light.)
3. Explain what location is best for that window. (e.g. It's best suited for a living room.)

Conversation 2

Listen to the rest of the conversation. Write all the words you can hear. Compare and discuss with your partner. 33

```
Memo



```

1 Listen to the conversation again and write T if the statement is true or F if false.

1. Sherry suggests planning the electric wiring before discussing the lighting. ( )
2. The living room has a lot of light and air flow. ( )
3. Tom wants the bedroom to have bright lighting. ( )
4. There will be enough space to put lamps next to the bed. ( )
5. Sherry didn't bring the catalogues of lights today. ( )

2 Listen to the conversation again and write the answers to the questions below.

1. What are they talking about now?
   _____.

2. Why does Sherry suggest to install some downlights?
   _____.

3. What kind of lighting does Tom want in the bedroom?
   _____.

4. What does Sherry think is important about the lighting in the dining room?
   _____.

GOOD TO KNOW

Too dark? Too bright?

You may be surprised by the dim lighting in some homes in Western countries. The rooms are often lit by lamps such as floor lamps or reading lamps. Most rooms in Japanese houses have one very bright ceiling light. There are a variety of possible reasons for the difference in styles: lifestyle differences; sitting on chairs vs sitting on the floor; or the fact that rooms are smaller in Japan and have less need of light in the corners. Lighting the whole room with a single light is still very common in Japan. However, in recent years there has been a trend toward using indirect lighting, similar to Western countries.

Unit 8
SCALE & DIMENSION: Talking about sizes and shapes of furniture

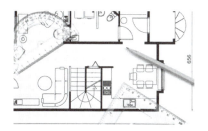

OBJECTIVES

Vocabulary: To learn different scales and shapes
Pronunciation: To practice /θ/ and /ð/
Grammar: To describe scale and dimension using countable and uncountable nouns
Conversation: To talk about scales and shapes of furniture

Vocabulary

1 Match the words and the meanings.

1. scale [ ]
2. dimension [ ]
3. proportion [ ]
4. length [ ]
5. width [ ]
6. depth [ ]
7. height [ ]
8. square [ ]
9. rectangle [ ]
10. circle [ ]
11. oval [ ]
12. diagram [ ]

a. 楕円	b. 深さ	c. 寸法	d. 正方形
e. 比率	f. 図	g. 幅	h. 高さ
i. 四角形	j. 長さ	k. 円	l. 縮尺

2 Complete the sentences using vocabulary above. Change the word form (plural, etc.) if necessary.

1. Each side of a _____ is the same length.
2. Please adjust the _____ of the chair so that your feet will touch the floor.
3. This _____ has a diameter of 20 cm.
4. The _____ shows different types of kitchen layouts.
5. The table is too big. It's not in _____ to the room.

【More Words】
 34

diameter 直径， radius 半径， outlet コンセント， feature 特徴， element 要素， appropriate 適切な， equivalent（価値・数量など）同等の， indicate 示す， six-seater 六人掛け， traffic 人の行き来， edges 端、角， scaled proportionally （縦横の）比率を変えずに拡大・縮小された， scale drawing 縮尺図面、特定の縮尺で描かれた図面， reduced scale of 1:100 (reduced scale of one to one hundred) 百分の一縮尺
shape の 名詞／形容詞：square/square, rectangle/rectangular, circle/circular, triangle/triangular, oval/oval

PRONUNCIATION

/θ/ and /ð/

These two sounds are ones that Japanese people have difficulty with. To form the /θ/ and /ð/ sounds place your tongue between your upper and lower teeth and move your tongue away to produce /θ/ or /ð/ sound. /θ/ and /ð/ are made in exactly the same way as each other. The only difference is that /θ/ is voiceless (no vocal cord vibration), but /ð/ is voiced (with vocal cord vibration).

1 Listen to the CD and practice pronouncing the words below.　　　　　　　　　35

1. leng<u>th</u>
2. dep<u>th</u>
3. wid<u>th</u>
4. clo<u>th</u>ing
5. smoo<u>th</u>
6. lea<u>th</u>er

2 Listen to the CD and circle the word you hear in each pair of words.　　　　　36

1. think / sink
2. bath / bus
3. path / pass
4. those / dose
5. though / dough
6. there / dare

GRAMMAR POINT

Countable and uncountable nouns

物事の数や量について話してみよう：**Talking about the number/amount of things for countable**（可算名詞）**and uncountable**（不可算名詞）**nouns**

"Table" に "a" を付け忘れたり "two table" にしてみたり、「この単語は数えられたっけ？」と可算名詞と不可算名詞の区別はわかりにくいですね。「可算名詞は絵に描きやすく、不可算名詞は絵にしにくいもの」とイメージすると良いかもしれません。ここでは、物事の数や両に絞って可算＆不可算名詞を復習しましょう。

● 可算名詞（描きやすいもの）

outlet, pillar, house, apartment, building, pipe, client, architect, resident, project, feature, section, element など。

What **elements** are combined in the study of architecture at university?
Corbusier thought that **a house** should be a machine to live in.

● 不可算名詞（描きにくいもの：液体、気体、素材、概念、固有の形が不明確なもの）

wood, gas, air, smoke, steam, water, furniture, coal, wind, snow, advice, information, evidence, electricity, news など。

Philosophy is not the most important subject in university architecture courses.
Society influenc**es** architects.
Architects influence **society**.

● 可算名詞であり不可算名詞でもある（意味により異なる）

family, audience, society など。

可算名詞：an academic **society**：学術学会（会、協会、団体を表す）
不可算名詞：human **society**：人間社会（組織体としての社会を表す）

1 Choose the appropriate words.

1. Stan would like to get some (advices, advice) from his project team.
2. How many inches are in a (foot, feet)?
3. Twelve (inches, inch) are equivalent to one foot.
4. Our clients prefer having a rectangular house under 1,000 square (feet, foot).

2 Complete the sentences using the words in parentheses.

1. 各フロアに何世帯ありますか？

   (How, are, each, many, units, there, on, floor)?

   _____?

2. あなたのアパートにはいくつの家具がありますか？

   (How, much, your, furniture, does, have, apartment)?

   _____?

3. プロジェクトチームのメンバーは、顧客の個人情報を厳重に取り扱わなければいけない。

   (All, handling, members, of, need to, the project, be careful,
   clients' personal information).

   _____.

4. このアパートには36世帯が住んでいます。

   (There, this, in, are, 36 families, apartment building).

   _____.

Conversation 1

1 Practice the conversation in pairs or groups.

Mika: Sherry, Tom emailed me the list of furniture he wants for the penthouse units.
Sherry: Can I see it? Oh, he indicated the size of the furniture as well.
Mika: Yes, he did. Some pieces seem too big though.
Sherry: I agree. The dining table isn't the right size.
Mika: Are you going to suggest a smaller dining table?
Sherry: Yes. Tom says he wants a 200 cm x 95 cm rectangular dining table for his unit. The width is OK, but it's too long. Do they really need a table for six?
Mika: Tom told me that they often have friends over for dinner, so he wants a six-seater table.
Sherry: But their dining room is 335 cm x 440 cm. The table needs to suit the space.
Mika: Yes.
Sherry: They need space to pull out chairs and also have enough room for people to walk around it.
Mika: How much space around the table do you think is needed?
Sherry: I would say at least 90 cm or ideally more than 100 cm.
Mika: That sounds reasonable. Why don't you talk with Tom with the scale drawing you made?
Sherry: Yes. I'm going to meet him tomorrow anyway. Once he sees it, I think he will understand.

2 Work with a partner. Fill in the blanks and make your own short conversation.

A: Tom emailed me the list of furniture he wants for the ____(place/room)____.
B: Let me see. Oh, he indicated the size of the furniture as well.
A: Yes, he did. Some pieces seem too ____(big/small)____ though.
B: Which one do you think is too ____(big/small)____?
A: I think ____(the table, etc.)____ should be _____.

Activity (Pair work)

The illustration below show the sizes of bed mattress in US sizes. Talk about different sized beds using the following sentence pattern.

A: The mattress is _____ mm long and _____ mm wide.
B: That's a _____-size mattress.

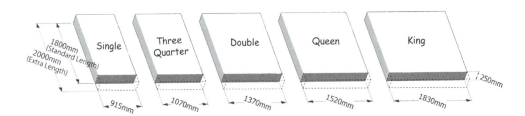

52

Unit 8

Conversation 2

Listen to the rest of the conversation. Write all the words you can hear. Compare and discuss with your partner. 38

Memo

1 Listen to the conversation again and write T if the statement is true or F if false.
1. Sherry and Tom are discussing the furniture for the penthouse units. (   )
2. The scale drawing Sherry shows is 1:200. (   )
3. Sherry's suggestion is a larger dining table for Tom. (   )
4. Sherry suggested a square dining table for Tom's daughter's unit. (   )

2 Listen to the conversation again and write the answers to the questions below.
1. What is the size of the dining table Sherry suggests to Tom?

   _____.

2. How many people can be seated at the table?

   _____.

3. What is the size of the dining table for Tom's daughter's unit?

   _____.

4. What shape of coffee table is suggested for Tom's daughter's living room?

   _____.

53

GOOD TO KNOW
USCS and the Metric System

Historically, different countries have used different systems of measuring length, weight, area, and volume. The United States Customary System (USCS), also known as the yard-pound system, is used in America and a few other countries. For measuring length, the USCS system uses the inch, foot, yard, and mile; for weight it uses the ounce and pound. In most other countries, including Japan, the metric system has become the standard. For length, the metric system uses the millimeter, meter, and kilometer; for weight it uses grams and kilograms. In general, the areas of houses in America are measured in square feet, but in Japan they are measured in square meters.

Length: 1" (inch) ≒ 25.4 mm (millimeters), 1' (foot) ≒ 30 cm (centimeters)
1 mi (mile) ≒ 1.6 km (kilometers)

Weight: 1 oz. (ounce) ≒ 28 g (grams), 1 lb. (pound) ≒ 454 g (grams)

Area: 10 ft² (square feet) ≒ 0.92 m² (square meters)

Volume: 10 ft³ (cubic feet) = 0.28 m³ (cubic meters)

Unit 9
COLORS & MATERIALS: Talking about preferences in colors and materials

OBJECTIVES

Vocabulary: To learn words describing colors
Pronunciation: To practice reduced sounds
Grammar: To describe colors and materials using verbs used as adjectives
Conversation: To talk about the material and color of kitchen cabinets

Vocabulary

1 Match the words and the meanings.

1. rental unit [   ]
2. a sense of [   ]
3. cleanliness [   ]
4. prefer [   ]
5. traditional [   ]
6. modern [   ]
7. solid (color) [   ]
8. pattern [   ]
9. wooden [   ]
10. shades [   ]
11. marble [   ]
12. go well with [   ]

a. 無地	b. 伝統的	c. ～という感覚	d. 木製の
e. 大理石	f. 近代的	g. 賃貸マンション	h. ～と合う
i. 清潔さ	j. 柄	k. より好む	l. (濃淡の) 色合

2 Complete the sentences using the vocabulary above. Change the word form (plural, etc.) if necessary.

1. There are different _____ of green, from dark to light.
2. I want the countertop to be made of _____ because it's smooth and stylish.
3. Which do you _____, solid or patterned wallpaper?
4. How many _____ are there in this apartment building?
5. White furniture gives a sense of _____ to the room.

55

【More Words】

polished 磨かれた；光沢のある， lightly 薄く、軽く， stained 着色された， soothing 落ち着かせる， energetic 活動的な、エネルギッシュな， let me know 知らせてください， wallpaper 壁紙， though ～だけれど， carpeted カーペットが敷かれた， wall-to-wall 床全面， hardwood floor 堅木の床：oak, cherry, ebony, mahogany など， plank 厚板， lumber 木材， texture 質感， arrange the day and time 日程調整をする， actual 実際の， pick you up 迎えに行く， country-style カントリー調， traditional 伝統的な， marble 大理石， except ～ ～以外， catalogue カタログ， tiled walls タイル張りの壁， pattern 柄， solid 無地；個体の，中まで詰まった， warp 伸縮による木の反り、歪み

PRONUNCIATION

The sounds you may not hear but are there

When a word ends with a consonant, the consonant is usually not audible. For example, *colored* may sound like *color* because you don't hear the /d/ at the end. However, your mouth should be in the form of articulation for the sound. Hold it for a while.

1 Listen to the CD and practice the phrases below. Pay attention to the underlined part.

1. colore<u>d</u> white /kʌ́ləd wáɪt/   *color white /kʌ́lɚ wáɪt/
2. staine<u>d</u> dark /stéɪnd dáɚk/   *stain dark /stéɪn dáɚk/
3. patterne<u>d</u> tiles /pǽənd táɪlz/   * pattern tiles /pǽən táɪlz/
4. I'<u>d</u> like /aɪd láɪk/   I like /aɪ láɪk/

2 Listen to the CD and circle the words you hear.

1. textured tiles / *texture tiles
2. satisfied customers / satisfy customers
3. carpeted floor / *carpet floor
4. I'll wait / I wait
5. polished wood / polish wood
6. I'd like / I like

(*-marked phrases may not be grammatical)

GRAMMAR POINT

Verbs used as adjective

色や質感について話してみよう：**Talking about colors and materials using *present/past participle verbs as adjectives*** （分詞の形容詞的用法）

"~ing" にするか "~ed" にするか迷うことがありますよね。分詞とはこのように動詞の形を変えて、形容詞としての働きをする便利や役割をします。なぜなら、現在分詞 "~ing" と過去分詞 "~ed" がそれぞれ形容詞としてその前後の名詞を修飾することができるからです。通常、現在分詞は「〜している」、過去分詞は「〜された」の意味で修飾します。ここでは、主に色や質感を表す分詞を復習しましょう。

- 「〜している」（現在分詞）
  He is working on a projects in **developing** countries.

- 「〜された、〜される」（過去分詞）
  I want to have **carpeted** floors for the bedroom.

語順は：

1) 分詞1語で名詞を修飾する場合　→　現在 / **過去分詞**＋名詞
   We requested the repair of the **broken** window.

2) 分詞の他に1語でも余分な語が付く場合　→　名詞＋現在 / **過去分詞**＋α
   We requested the repair of the window **broken** in the storm.

1 Complete the sentences using the words in parentheses.

1. 白い家具は清潔感があります。
   (Furniture, white, colored, cleanliness, gives, a, sense, of).

   _____.

2. 私は緑色で塗られた部屋が好きです。
   (I, the, like, room, green, painted).

   _____.

3. 父親は光沢のある木目の床がお気に入りです。
   (My, father, polished wood, likes, floors).

   _____.

4. タイル張りのお風呂は素敵に見えます。
   (Tiled, in, look, walls, stylish, the bathroom).

   _____.

5. リビングルームに柄のある壁紙を貼りたいです。
   (We, for, want to, patterned wallpapers, have, the living room).

   _____.

Conversation 1

1 Practice the conversation in pairs or groups.

Sherry: Let's decide on the material and color of the kitchen cabinets.
Tom: Sure. For the rental units, I'm thinking of having white colored wooden cabinets.
Sherry: That's good. White gives a sense of cleanliness and space. As for the penthouse units, which do you prefer, traditional or modern kitchens?
Tom: More like traditional, I guess.
Sherry: How about brown cabinets then? Here are the color samples.
Tom: Wow, there are many different shades of brown!
Sherry: Yes, there are all kinds of brown. Some are the natural wood, and some are stained.
Tom: My wife wants to have a country-style kitchen.
Sherry: How about lightly stained brown, then?
Tom: Does it go well with marble? She wants to use marble for the countertops.
Sherry: No problem. White or grey marble will go well with light brown cabinets.
Tom: White or grey? Let me ask my wife which color she prefers.

2 Work with a partner. Fill in the blanks and make your own short conversation.

A: Let's decide on the material and color of _____.
B: Sure. For the _____, I'm thinking of _____.
A: That's good. The color _____ gives a sense of _____.
B: You're right.

> Color terms: white, black, grey, pink, yellow, brown, blue, light blue, green, light green, red, purple, orange, beige, silver metallic, gold, lavender, etc.
> Sense of…: energy, calmness, peace, comfort, quiet, relaxation, warmth, creativity, etc.

Activity (Group work)

1 Fill in the blanks and make your own sentence.

e.g. I like white. White gives a sense of cleanliness and space.

I like _____. _____ gives a sense of _____.

2 Walk around the class and ask three people about their favorite colors. Write the reasons why they like the color.

Student name	The reason why he/she likes the color
	The color _____ gives a sense of _____.
	The color _____ gives a sense of _____.
	The color _____ gives a sense of _____.

Conversation 2

Listen to the rest of the conversation. Write all the words you can hear. Compare and discuss with your partner. 43

Memo

1 Listen to the conversation again and write T if the statement is true or F if false.
1. Tom is planning to have wall-to-wall carpeting for the rental units. (   )
2. Tom and his wife want to have hardwood floors for their penthouse unit. (   )
3. Tom and his daughter want to have solid wallpaper for their living rooms. (   )
4. Tom will have time to go to the wallpaper shop with Sherry tomorrow. (   )
5. Sherry is going to pick up Tom in the early afternoon. (   )

2 Listen to the conversation again and fill in the blanks below.
1. Tom and Sherry are talking about the _____ and _____ of the living room.
2. Sherry thinks that a soft, _____ floor is safe for small children.
3. Tom's daughter thinks that _____ is easier to keep clean.
4. Tom wants to have _____ for both penthouse units.

GOOD TO KNOW
Engineered Wood

Do you know the word *engineered wood*? It's also called composite wood or manufactured board. Layers of wood materials are glued together and compressed into board. Engineered woods are tested to meet quality standards. As for the material of flooring, engineered wood tends to be less expensive and generally stronger than natural woods, especially against moisture. Unlike wood, it doesn't warp or bend out of shape. It's also better for the environment because it's made from a mix of small pieces of wood. This means that it helps reduce cutting down the trees from old growth forests.

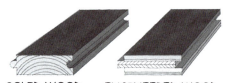

SOLID WOOD   ENGINEERED WOOD

Unit 10
SUSTAINABLE DESIGN: Talking about environmentally friendly designs

OBJECTIVES

Vocabulary: To learn the words describing saving energy
Pronunciation: To practice the [ng]-sound
Grammar: To make suggestions using auxiliary verbs
Conversation: To talk about environmentally friendly designs

Vocabulary

1 Match the words and the meanings.

1. sustainable [ ]
2. guarantee [ ]
3. economical [ ]
4. comply [ ]
5. environmentally friendly [ ]
6. rainwater tank [ ]
7. device [ ]
8. reduce [ ]
9. consumption [ ]
10. law [ ]
11. dual flush [ ]
12. household [ ]

```
a. 削減する         b. 家庭           c. 経済的          d. 機器・機械
e. 環境にやさしい   f. ダブル水洗     g. ～に従う        h. 法律
I. 保証する         j. 持続可能な     k. 雨水タンク      l. 消費
```

2 Complete the sentences using the vocabulary above. Change the word form (plural, etc.) if necessary.

1. Architects consider _____ design as part of environmentally friendly construction.
2. We have to _____ with the building codes when building a house.
3. The number of toilets with _____ is increasing in Japan.
4. Although it may be less _____, recycled materials are more sustainable.
5. We should _____ the amount of water we use because it's very dry this year.

【More Words】

ordinary 一般的な, per minute 毎分, water-saving 節水の, water pressure 水圧, affect 影響する, usage 使用, sustainable design 環境に配慮したデザイン, arrangement of rooms 屋根の配置, sizing of windows 窓サイズの検討

Environment-friendly construction techniques:

using recycled materials リサイクル材料の使用, installing solar panels ソーラーパネルの設置, installing a green roof グリーンルーフの設置, adding insulation to exterior walls and roofs 外壁と屋根の断熱材使用, installing water-saving fixtures 節水器具の設置, installing a grey-water tank (system) 雑用水貯水タンクの設置, planting trees 植栽, using paint and sealant with low VOC 揮発性有機化合物 (volatile organic compound) 低含量ペイントの使用, using materials with low formaldehyde levels 低ホルムアルデヒド材料の使用, installing sunshades 日よけの設置, using LED light bulbs LED 電球の使用, installing a dimmer 光調整器の設置, installing a heat exchanger 熱交換器の設置, 他

PRONUNCIATION

The ng-sound, /ŋ/ (not /gʊ/)

Japanese people tend to pronounce the words like *sing* as /síŋgʊ/, but the correct pronunciation is /síŋ/. You don't hear a /g/ sound but may hear more like an /n/ or Japanese 「ん」. When you produce the /ŋ/ sound, keep your lips apart and say 「ん」 with your tongue in the position of producing a /g/ sound. When you produce an /n/ sound, the tip of your tongue is placed behind your teeth, but your tongue is lowered and not touching anywhere for /ŋ/.

1 Listen to the CD and circle the word you hear in each pair of words.

1. sun / sung
2. thin / thing
3. win / wing
4. kin / king
5. ton / tong
6. ran / rang

2 Practice pronouncing the following phrases in which the words ending in /ŋ/ are followed by a word. You will notice that there is no /g/ sound there either.

1. sing a song
2. wrong address
3. King Andrew
4. long distance
5. using amenities
6. dining table

GRAMMAR POINT

Auxiliary verbs

義務を表す "have to" と意見を表す "should"：Understanding the nuances of obligation/suggestion using "have to" and "should" (助動詞)

「絶対に時間通りに来てください（遅れるな！）。」と念を押したい時、次のどちらの文を使いますか？ "You have to be on time." ですか？それとも "You should be on time." ですか？ニュアンスが難しいですね。Have to「〜しなければいけなない（義務・命令）」、should「〜したらどうですか（提案・意見）」です。このユニットでは、「持続可能な環境」をテーマとし、"have to" と "should" の違いを復習しましょう。

- have to: 〜しなければならない（義務・命令）

  *have to は、must と置き換えることができます。

  We **have to** finish the project by the end of the year as we guaranteed it in the contract.

- should: 〜したらどうですか（提案・意見）

  **should は、could と置き換えることができます。

  You **should** take a look through the catalogue to see the different types of faucets.

  If you want the room to look more spacious, you **should** paint it a light color.

1 Complete the sentences using the words in parentheses.

1. ソーラパネルと雨水用のタンクの取り付けたらどうですか？

   (We, a, installing, rainwater tank, should, consider, solar panels, and).

   _____.

2. 建築家は環境規制に従わなければいけません。

   (Architects, with, have to, comply, environmental regulations).

   _____.

3. 節水のために歯を磨いているときには水を止めるべきです。

   (We, the water, should, turn off, while, to, we, brush, our teeth, save water).

   _____.

4. 節水するため、すべての新しいトイレはデュアル洗浄（一回に流す水量の大小が選べるタイプ）にすべきです。

   (All, reduce, new toilets, dual flush, have to, be, to, water consumption).

   _____.

5. 消費電力を抑えるために、LED の電球を使用した方が良いです。

   (To, LED light bulbs, save, we, electricity, should, use).

   _____.

Conversation 1

1 Practice the conversation in pairs or groups.

Tom: We should think about ways to use environmentally friendly designs in the project.

Mika: Yes. Using water-saving devices is one good way. They reduce water consumption a lot. Ed is in charge of the plumbing. He can tell you more about it.

Tom: OK, thanks.

Ed: First, let's work on saving water in the toilet. About 30% of water used in homes is for the toilet.

Tom: Wow, 30%? That's a lot.

Ed: Actually, from next year the law will change. All new toilets have to be dual flush.

Tom: I see. Even if we don't have to install it, I think we should.

Ed: OK. Another way to reduce water use is to choose water-saving shower heads and faucets. You could consider a rainwater tank as well.

Tom: I see. We should save water where we can. It's good for the environment and it's economical.

2 Work with a partner. Fill in the blanks and make your own short conversation.

A: We should think about being environmentally friendly.

B: Yes. One good way is installing/reducing/recycling _____.

A: Yes, installing/reducing/recycling _____ will be good for _____!

Activity

Using the words introduced in [More Words], suggest a sustainable design strategy. Fill in blank 1 with the choices below to explain how the strategy contributes to the environment. Make a short conversation with your partner. Share your conversation in class.

A: We should think about sustainable design in architecture.

B: You're right. I think _____ is important.

A: What is the advantage of that?

B: It helps ____1____ .

Choices for 1:

a. reduce the consumption of natural resources (energy, material)

b. provide a healthy and comfortable environment for occupants in and around the building

c. reduce the negative impacts of pollution or CO_2 emissions on our natural environment

d. _____ (*My own reason*)

Conversation 2

Listen to the rest of the conversation. Write all the words you can hear. Compare and discuss with your partner. 🎧 48

Memo

1 Listen to the conversation again and write T if the statement is true or F if false.
1. Tom and Ed are discussing where to install faucets. (　)
2. Ed recommends a way to save water in the shower. (　)
3. Tom agrees to use a water-saving showerhead. (　)
4. Tom and Ed discuss ways to save water other than the bathroom. (　)
5. Tom decided to install a rainwater tank. (　)

2 Listen to the conversation again and fill in the blanks below.
1. Tom and Ed are talking about _____.
2. More than _____ of household water is used for showers.
3. A water-saving shower uses about _____ of water per minute.
4. When you choose a faucet, you need to think about water usage, _____ and _____.
5. Ed suggests that rainwater could be used for _____ or flushing the toilets.

GOOD TO KNOW
Water

Different environments and climates create needs for different laws. In most of Japan, water is plentiful, so people tend not to think very seriously about saving water. In contrast, California does not get much rain, and water is precious. For example, Los Angeles gets only 384 mm of rain in an average year, whereas Tokyo gets 1530 mm. In California, it is important not to waste water. As a result, in California, a law was passed in 2015 which banned the sale of toilets that used more than 1.28 gallons (4.8 liters) of water per flush. Another example of sustainable water policies is Singapore. Singapore is a small island which used to rely on importing water from other countries to meet local needs. In recent years though, the government of Singapore has aimed to have water self-sufficiency. Because of this, Singapore has invested a lot of money in water collection and purification facilities. Singapore is one of the few countries that separates rain water collection from storm water collection. Stormwater is collected and treated until it is safe for human consumption. Now, the Public Utility Board of Singapore supplies treated, used water called "NEWater." The total capacity of the water treatment plants currently has the potential to supply about 40% of Singapore's water usage. All places need to look at their environment to determine what sustainability programs are best for them.

HOW TO SAVE WATER

Unit 11
NATURAL HAZARDS: Talking about protecting buildings from natural hazards

OBJECTIVES

Vocabulary: To learn words describing natural hazards
Pronunciation: To learn and practice /a/, /e/, /i/, /o/, /u/, and /æ/
Grammar: To describe natural hazards using conditional sentences
Conversation: To talk about the durability of a building

Vocabulary

1 Match the words and meanings.

1. durability [   ]
2. reinforced [   ]
3. mudslide [   ]
4. seismic [   ]
5. strict [   ]
6. hurricane [   ]
7. absorb [   ]
8. surrounded [   ]
9. reclaimed [   ]
10. resistant [   ]
11. blow off [   ]
12. extreme [   ]

a. 〜に囲まれた	b. 極度の	c. 地すべり	d. ハリケーン
e. 厳しい	f. 地震の	g. 吸収する	h. 永続性、耐久性
i. 埋め立てられた	j. 抵抗力／耐久性のある	k. 吹きとばす	l. 補強された

2 Complete the sentences using vocabulary above. Change the word form (plural, etc.) if necessary.

1. This concrete is _____ so that it's stronger.
2. The big hurricane may _____ the roofs of old houses.
3. This system will _____ the vibration caused by earthquakes.
4. This area is _____ by hills, so we worry about mudslides.
5. Japan's building code is very _____ about earthquake safety.

【More Words】

briefly 簡潔に，consider 考える，resistance 耐性，disaster 災害，earthquake 地震，property 土地建物，earthquake resistance 耐震性，cracked ひびが入った，withstand 耐える，building code 建築基準法，collapse 崩壊する，no longer ~ もはや~でない，vibration 振動，reclaimed land 埋立地，liquefaction 液状化，solid 頑丈な，firmly しっかりと，attached 取り付けてある，vibration control structure 制振構造，earthquake resistant structure 耐震構造，seismic isolation structure 免震構造

Hurricanes, typhoons, and cyclones:

Hurricanes, typhoons, and cyclones are the same weather phenomenon. They are called "hurricanes" when they occur in the Atlantic and Northeast Pacific, "typhoons" in the Northwest Pacific, and a "cyclones" in the South Pacific and Indian Ocean.

PRONUNCIATION

Tense vowels and lax vowels

There are tense vowels and lax vowels in English. /i/, /e/, /u/, /o/, /a/, and /ɔ/ are called tense vowels. They are slightly longer, and you may feel that they are slightly stronger than lax vowels. Lax vowels are more like "weaker and shorter" vowels. Those are /ɪ/, /ɛ/, /ʊ/, /ə/ and /æ/. In most cases, you don't have to worry too much about a vowel being tense or lax, but there are some words which are difficult for Japanese learners of English. Let's practice /u/ and /ʊ/ here.

		Front	Central	Back
High	Tense	i (beat)		u (boot)
	Lax	ɪ (bit)		ʊ (book)
Mid	Tense	e (bait)	ʌ (but)	o (boat)
	Lax	ɛ (bet)	ə (about)	ɔ (paw)*
Low		æ (bat)		ɑ (pot)

*(not in all dialects)

http://pages.uoregon.edu/l150web/vowel.html

1 Listen to the CD and practice the paired words below.

1. fool / full   2. pool / pull   3. food / foot   4. Luke / look   5. soot / suit

2 Listen to the CD again and circle the word you hear.

1. fool / full   2. pool / pull   3. food / foot   4. Luke / look   5. soot / suit

GRAMMAR POINT

Conditionals

自然災害などの起こりうることを話してみよう：**Talking about conditional or imaginary situations**（仮定法）

「もし〜したら、〜だろうに」や「もし〜していたら、〜だっただろうに」など事実ではない主観的な想像や仮定の話をする時に仮定法を用います。ここでは自然災害などの起こりうる話題に焦点をあて、仮定法を復習しましょう。

- 現在の事実に反する仮想→過去形（仮定法過去）：もし〜なら ... だろうに
  If there were stricter building regulations, there would be less damage in an earthquake.

- 過去の事実に反する仮想→過去完了形（仮定法過去完了）：もし〜だったら ... だっただろうに
  If we had known it was reclaimed land, we wouldn't have bought a house here.

1 Complete the sentences using the words in the parentheses.

1. もしその技師がその窓を補強したほうが良いと言ってくれなかったら、壊れていただろう。
   (If, hadn't, the engineer, advised us, the windows, to reinforce, the windows, might have, blown out).

   _____.

2. もしそんなに雨が降らなかったら、土砂崩れも起きなかったかもしれない。
   (If, might not, there, hadn't been, so, a mudslide, much rain, have happened).

   _____.

3. 海岸に近かったら、津波を心配しなくてはいけないだろう。
   (If, the coast, we, were, on, we, would, tsunami, have to, think, about).

   _____.

4. 台風に関しての情報があれば、損害を防げたかもしれない。
   (If, information, we, had had, could have reduced, about the typhoon, we, the damage).

   _____.

Conversation 1

1 Practice the conversation in pairs or groups.

Brian: Let me explain briefly about the durability of this building.
Tom: Yes, please.
Brian: Durability means how resistant the building is to extreme weather and natural disasters such as earthquakes, snow storms, hurricanes, and tsunami.
Tom: I understand, but we don't get snow here and we are too far from the coast for a tsunami. But we need to think about hurricanes, don't we? How do you make the building more resistant to hurricanes?
Brian: One of the things we do for houses is that we limit the size of the windows. We also reinforce the area around the window frames.
Tom: I see. Are we going to do that on this project, too?
Brian: No. That's for houses as I said. We don't have to worry about hurricane resistance for a reinforced concrete building like yours. The walls are very solid and the roof is firmly attached.

2 Fill in the blanks and make your own short conversation with a partner. Change the roles and make another conversation.

(First time)
A: What kind of natural hazards do you have to worry about in your area?
B: We need to worry about _____.
A: How do you prepare for that?
B: We _____.
   If _____, _____.

(Second time)
B: What kind of natural hazards do you have to worry about in your area?
A: We need to worry about _____.
B: How do you prepare for that?
A: We _____.
   If _____, _____.

3 From the conversation above, find answers to the following questions.

1. What does "durability" mean?
   _____.

2. What examples of extreme weather are given?
   _____.

3. What natural disasters are mentioned?
   _____.

4. Why doesn't Tom have to worry about hurricane resistance?
   _____.

Conversation 2

Listen to the rest of the conversation. Write all the words you can hear. Compare and discuss with your partner. 🎧 53

> Memo

1 Listen to the conversation again and write T if the statement is true or F if false.
1. Tom and Brian are discussing natural disasters. ( )
2. Tom asks about tsunami protection. ( )
3. The local area gets earthquakes. ( )
4. Brian explains earthquake protection. ( )
5. Tom is satisfied with Brian's explanation. ( )

2 Listen to the conversation again and fill in the blanks below.
1. The local _____ includes seismic standards.
2. The walls, beams, and _____ need to be stronger to reduce the effect of earthquakes.
3. Seismic isolators are like rubber _____.
4. Brian says that the isolators are not really necessary in a _____ structure building with five stories.
5. Isolators reduce damage inside the building, but they are very _____.

71

GOOD TO KNOW

Loads for Structural Design

When buildings are designed, the structural engineer has to consider ways to make the building strong. The structure of a building has to withstand various loads. For example, an engineer has to design building so that the structure can support the weight of furniture and people inside the building. The building also needs to be able to resist external forces. You have probably heard of buildings collapsing under snow. This is an example of the kind of force that the structural engineer needs to think about. It is necessary for protecting human life and property. The examples below show the different kinds of loads that are considered in the structure of a building.

- Dead Load: Weight of the structure itself and objects attached to the building
- Live Load: Weight of objects and people in the building
- Snow Load: Weight of snow on the building
- Wind Load: Wind pressure acting on the building
- Earthquake Load: Seismic force acting on the building during an earthquake

Unit 12
URBAN DESIGN: Talking about infrastructure planning

OBJECTIVES

Vocabulary: To learn words related to infrastructure
Pronunciation: To practice the rhythm of English
Grammar: To talk about urban design using passive voice
Conversation: To talk about the basics of urban planning

Vocabulary

1 Match the words and Japanese meanings.

1. community [ ]
2. commute [ ]
3. infrastructure [ ]
4. pedestrian [ ]
5. mixed use [ ]
6. transportation [ ]
7. reduce [ ]
8. compact [ ]
9. construction [ ]
10. public [ ]
11. destroy [ ]
12. emission [ ]

  a. 運送   b. 破壊する   c. インフラストラクチャー   d. 建造物
  e. 複合用途 f. 地域社会   g. 減らす   h. コンパクト
  i. 歩行者   j. 公共   k. 通勤・通学する   l. 排出

2 Complete the sentences using the vocabulary above. Change the word form (plural, etc.) if necessary.

1. Watch out! There is a _____ crossing the street.
2. _____ means the physical structures that make a city function including transport, communication and energy systems.
3. Tokyo has an excellent public _____ system, so you don't really need to own a car.
4. Instead of using an air conditioner, using a natural flow of air will _____ the use of electricity.
5. The local _____ holds many events each year.

73

【More Words】 54

urban planning 都市計画, promote 促進する, resident 住人, agency 主体, overall 全体の, water system 上下水道システム, exactly 正確に、まさに, individual 個々／個々の、個人／個人の, urban planners 都市プランナー, trend 傾向, mixed-use development 複合開発, standard of living 生活水準, commuting time 通勤時間, quality of life 生活の質, concrete 具体的な

PRONUNCIATION

Rhythm of English

Japanese people tend to speak English in a flat, monotonous tone. As you have practiced in earlier units, English places stress on certain syllables, and content words (the words carrying important information) are pronounced strongly and clearly. By having clear stress within words and making a distinction between strong (i.e. louder, longer, and higher in pitch) and weak pronunciation(i.e. softer, shorter) of words, you can create a natural rhythm when you speak.

1 Stress the words in bold as you read the following sentences. 55

1. Could you **tell me** about **urban planning**?
2. I've **never done** a **large scale project**.
3. **Recently** there has been a **trend** towards **mixed development**.
4. The **idea** is to **have** a **compact city**.
5. It is **better** for the **environment**.

2 Read the following words (A) and sentences (B) with a partner. You should finish reading (A) and (B) at the same time. Underlines indicate groups of words.

1. (A)　　　　tell　　　　urban planning?
   (B) <u>Could you tell me</u> <u>about urban planning</u>?

2. (A)　　idea　　　have　　compact city.
   (B) <u>The idea</u> <u>is to have</u> <u>a compact</u> city.

3. (A)　　　better　　　　environment.
   (B) <u>It is better</u> <u>for the environment</u>.

GRAMMAR POINT

Passive Voice

「〜される」を使って都市計画について話してみよう：Talking about urban design using passive voice（受動態）

「主語が何かの行動をする」文章を、能動態といい、動作の受け手を主語にした文が受動態（受け身）です。同じ意味で二通りの文が作れます。基本的な形は「主語＋ be 動詞＋過去分詞＋ by〜」で「〜される」と訳しますね。ここでは、「〜される」を使用して都市計画について話してみましょう。

- 能動態　（A が B を〜する）
  <u>The road construction</u> will destroy *the forest*.
  　　　A　　　　　　　　B

Unit 12

● 受動態 （B が A に〜される）

The forest will **be destroyed by** the road construction.
　　B　　　　　　　　　　　　　A

▶ 一般的な主語の場合、また、主語よりも動詞を強調したいときには by 以下が訳されることがあります。受動態では主語が省略されることが多いです。

受動態：The water pipes can **be placed** under the roads.
能動態：(Construction workers) can place the water pipes under the roads.
　　　　　　主語　　　　　　　　動詞

受動態：Mixed-use development is **being promoted**
能動態：(The local government is) promoting mixed-use development.

受動態：The town was designed so that residents have easy access to public transportation.
能動態：(Some people - *we don't need to know who*) designed the town so that residents have easy access to public transportation.

受動態：The land was zoned for residential use.
能動態：(Someone or some agency - *not important who*) zoned the land for residential use.

▶ 主語があっても動詞が強調される場合もあります。

受動態：The overall plans are being made by Mika.
能動態：Mika is making the overall plans.
　　　　主語　　動詞

受動態：The interiors are being designed by Sherry.
能動態：Sherry is designing the interiors.

1 Complete the sentences using the words in parentheses.

1. 複合開発は仕事場までの交通量を減らしてくれるでしょう。

   (Mixed-use development, for transportation, reduce, the use of cars, will, to the workplace).

   _____.

2. ミカはトムにインフラストラクチャーや土地利用はとても重要だと伝えました。

   (Mika, really, told, that, infrastructure and land use, Tom, are, important).

   _____.

3. エドは上下水道システムを計画している。

   (Ed, water, the, planning, system, is).

   _____.

4. 良い都市計画によって移動時間やCO₂排出量を削減することができる。
   (Travel time, can, and, good, by, CO₂ emissions, be reduced, urban, planning).

   _____.

5. コンパクトシティでは施設が互いに密接している。
   (Facilities, in, near, are located, each other, a compact city).

   _____.

Conversation 1

1 Practice the conversation in pairs or groups.

Tom: Could you tell me about urban planning? I'm interested in learning more about it for future projects.

Mika: Sure, but what exactly do you want to know?

Tom: I've built some condominium buildings, but I've never done a large scale project. So, I'd appreciate it if you could tell me a bit about the basics of urban planning.

Mika: Well, with urban planning, the first thing you need to think about is planning the infrastructure for the area.

Tom: I see, so you mean before you think about individual buildings, you need to think about the systems.

Mika: Yes, exactly. We need to think about the infrastructure before the buildings.

Tom: Such as roads and public transportation?

Mika: Not only that. We have to think about water, electricity, gas, and communication systems such as the Internet and telephone as well.

2 Work with a partner and make questions using words that appear in Conversation 1. Answer the questions using the phrases in the box below.

A: What does _____ mean?
B: It means _____.

> 1. the planning and designing of buildings, roads, and services in town
> 2. a building containing a number of individually owned apartments
> 3. a public system of vehicles such as buses and trains
> 4. the systems/network for telephone and the Internet

Conversation 2

Listen to the rest of the conversation. Write all the words you can hear. Compare and discuss with your partner. 🎧 57

Memo

1 Listen to the conversation again and write T if the statement is true or F if false.
1. Mixed development has become more popular recently. (   )
2. Mixed development means separating work and homes. (   )
3. Mixed development tries to create compact cities. (   )
4. Mixed development is good for people's daily life. (   )
5. People have more cars with mixed development. (   )

2 Listen to the conversation again and fill in the blanks below.
1. In addition to infrastructure, land usage and _____ are really important.
2. In mixed development, land for different purposes should be located _____.
3. Areas zoned for residential, commercial, and _____ purposes should be near each other.
4. Compact cities are better for the _____.
5. If people use their cars less, they can get more exercise and _____ in their community.

GOOD TO KNOW
Jane Jacobs and Urban Design

Good urban design occurs as a result of good planning. These days, many cities place great importance on making their city 'liveable', but it wasn't always this way. One of the most influential urban designers was Jane Jacobs (1916-2006). Jacobs became famous for her activism in the late 1950s. She stood up to protect her community, and her actions began to change people's thinking. Greenwich Park, near her home in New York city, was going to be turned into an expressway. Cars and big roads were seen as the way of the future. But Jacobs believed that an expressway through the park would be a disaster for community life. As a result, she gathered members of the community together to protest. In her plans, she emphasised the importance of pedestrians, and she worked to reduce the use of cars. She believed communities —not roads and buildings— should be the focus of urban life. Higher density and mixed land use would create an environment where people were familiar with the places where they lived, worked and played. This in turn would make the city safer, more interesting, and more vibrant. Although initially radical, Jacob's ideas have now become accepted by most urban planners.

http://www.janejacobswalk.org/about-jane-jacobs-walk/meet-jane-jacobs/

ホートン広瀬恵美子 **(Horton Hirose, Emiko)**：芝浦工業大学建築学部・共通教養外国語科目（教授）
　　BA（英語教授法 Teaching English as a Second Language）Hawaii Pacific University;　MA（言語学 Linguistics）University of Hawaii

恒安（堀川）眞佐 **(Tsuneyasu Horikawa, Masa)**：国際基督教大学（特任講師）
　　2019年4月より芝浦工業大学建築学部共通教養外国語科目（准教授）

Cecilia Smith Fujishima：白百合女子大学（講師）
　　BA (History), Sydney University;　MA (Global Studies), 上智大学

神谷英子 **(Kamiya, Hanako)**：日建設計コンストラクション・マネジメント株式会社；芝浦工業大学建築学部（非常勤講師）
　　BS（建築), 芝浦工業大学；MA (Architecture), Pratt Institute Graduate School of Architecture and Urban Design（米国）；米国および他の海外で9年間建設業務に従事．

著作権法上、無断複写・複製は禁じられています。

Basic English for Architecture —Listening & Speaking—　　[B-872]
建築を学ぶ人のための総合英語 ― リスニング＆スピーキング ―

1　刷　2019年 3月 28日

著　者	ホートン 広瀬 恵美子	Emiko Hirose Horton	
	恒安(堀川)眞佐	Tsuneyasu Horikawa, Masa	
	スミス 藤島 セシリア	Cecilia Smith Fujishima	
	神谷　英子	Hanako Kamiya	

発行者　　南雲　一範　　Kazunori Nagumo
発行所　　株式会社　南雲堂
　　　　　〒162-0801　東京都新宿区山吹町361
　　　　　NAN'UN-DO Co., Ltd.
　　　　　361 Yamabuki-cho, Shinjuku-ku, Tokyo 162-0801, Japan
　　　　　振替口座：00160-0-46863
　　　　　TEL: 03-3268-2311(営業部：学校関係)
　　　　　　　　03-3268-2384(営業部：書店関係)
　　　　　　　　03-3268-2387(編集部)
　　　　　FAX: 03-3269-2486
編集者　　加藤　敦
製　版　　橋本　佳子
装　丁　　銀月堂
検　印　　省　略
コード　　ISBN978-4-523-17872-9　C0082

Printed in Japan

E-mail　nanundo@post.email.ne.jp
URL　http://www.nanun-do.co.jp/

DESIGN ENGLISH
クリエイターのための闘う英語

高山靖子　亀井暁子　高瀬奈美　服部守悦　峯郁郎
Edward Sarich　Gary McLeod　Jack Ryan　Mark Sheehan　著

デザインの現場における経験をもとに
デザインを検討するときに使う言葉と
英会話のポイントをまとめた実践に
役立つ一冊！

定価（本体 2,800 円＋税）
A5 判 216 ページ＋別冊 86 ページ
ISBN978-4-523-26543-6　C0082

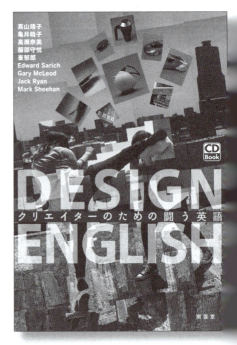

巻末にはデザイン校
の際に使用される、
辞書では調べにくい
語彙、表現を掲載

南雲堂

〒162-0801 東京都新宿区山吹町 361　　TEL 03-3268-2384　FAX 03-3260-5425